To Marc Corsini

May your life be charmed + your blessings never ending !

all my best,

Pam

Sept 97

# Remembering Your Destiny

## The Twelve Practices

# Remembering Your Destiny

## The Twelve Practices

### Pamela Murray

**BookPartners, Inc.**
*Wilsonville, Oregon*

***BookPartners, Inc.***
P.O. Box 922
Wilsonville, Oregon 97070

# Dedication

*To my incredible husband,*
*Larry, you're the greatest!*

# Acknowledgments

It's impossible to thank everyone individually who has contributed thus far to my journey, so please know that I am grateful to you all.

Thank you Michelle and Miriam for keeping me going when I wanted to quit. You're the best kickers of my behind I could ever have and show me the highest love and friendship by not accepting my excuses.

Charles and Helen, you've always been there for me and I am indebted to you beyond words. Here's to our eternal friendship. (And, I really do mean eternal!)

Steve and Randa, I love our long discussions and healing sessions. It's a wonder we've survived them. You give me so much insight and love.

Betty, thanks for getting me started on this book and for your loving friendship.

Thanks, Mom, Dad, Chris, Martha and the rest of the family for your unflagging support. I couldn't do this without you. I'm sure at many times you've regarded me in the same way Papa, my grandfather, described my grandma, "Highly intelligent but somewhat peculiar."

And, finally, to Larry. Yes, I know I dedicated the book to you, but I want to thank you again for literally making it possible for me to do what I do. You're my knight in shining armor!

# Table of Contents

# *Introduction*

When an artist paints a picture, he has a good idea of what it will look like when it is complete. He begins by priming the canvas to prepare it for the paint. He then roughs in the large areas, creating the "blueprint" for the finished piece.

Our lives are very much like that canvas. At the point of your soul's creation, whether you believe it was created when the sperm and egg joined or at the beginning of time, a "blueprint" unique to you was fashioned by the Great Artist. We all come into this life knowing at some level what our destiny is, what we were created to be. Unfortunately, we forget all too soon, spending much of our time stumbling around, struggling to fill in the details of the picture without ever checking the blueprint.

The great singer and minister, Charles King, calls us "Angels With Amnesia," who have forgotten that we were created in greatness, sent here to give form to our blueprint. The purpose of this book is to help you regain some of your lost memory, to recover from the "amnesia," and follow the plan laid out in your original design.

The twelve areas outlined in this book — The Twelve Practices — are designed to help you not only rediscover your natural pattern, but to help you get rid of the distractions that cloud your picture and instead set about living more in the flow of your divine design.

This book is spiritual in nature. As an ordained minister, I cannot separate the spiritual from the mundane. This is because a spiritual approach to life is far too practical to ignore. Rather than complicating life, as many believe, following a spiritual path in life actually serves to simplify it. By learning to live at this level, you will save time and money by listening to your inner guidance, and you will eliminate many of the emotional vampires which drain your life forces.

The exercises are designed to help you build the skills you need to create a more exciting, practical, and fun life. When your three-dimensional destiny finally emerges from the blueprint roughed out on the canvas, it is rich with the essence of the Designer.

Will you still have problems and trials? If my life is any example, yes. But I have a greater awareness of how to get through them. I'm learning my lessons more quickly now and from an ever higher perspective.

This book is not academic theory. It's about real life, real lessons, and real people. As with my first book, *The New Success: How To Redefine, Create and Survive Your Own Success,* you will find many stories about my own journey in this book. You will learn how I've applied these practices to my own life. You will also read stories about others who have applied the same principles and how they have been helped.

Many of the exercises are as old as mankind. Others have come to me from my inner source in response to my requests to help me or others learn how to apply these practices to our everyday lives.

We often think of Destiny simply as the means for our livelihood. Yet, that is but a small part of it. In fact, our careers may have little or nothing to do with our destiny.

Destiny has more to do with how we play our role in humanity.

It is not enough merely to recapture your original blueprint. It was never meant to sit on a shelf to be contemplated, nor were you meant to recline on your velvet pillow meditating on wondrous things. You were meant to act and do your part in fully expressing yourself while helping to make our planet a better place for all of us.

Destiny is that innate sense of purpose — a calling, a pull that is as ancient as the soul. Destiny has to do with our core purpose, the reason we chose to become human.

In its most basic form destiny is very simple. It has to do with the agreement, the "contract" made by the primordial soul. Destiny is not simply the lessons we need to learn, but also includes our role in the healing and furthering of the planet and the other beings on it.

As I've mentioned, Destiny may have little to do with your vocation, although a destiny properly remembered at the right time may lead you in the direction of a job that directly involves your purpose. But vocation is not the prime consideration in fully expressing one's destiny.

I suspect that, as an infant or small child, we may still be connected to our destiny and can still hear the voice of the Beloved whispering in our ear. But, as we age and our bodies become denser and our consciousness fills with the wonders of the earth, our connection with the language of Spirit weakens until, at some point, we cease to understand it and, finally, we no longer hear it at all.

There is, however, a part of us still searching for that lost voice. We're not always aware of it, but, sometimes, when the earth is still and we are alone with only our heart as company, we occasionally hear the voice whispering, "Come home, precious child. You are missed." And we wonder where home is.

And, sometimes, we know there is more than we're expressing, more that we need to be doing. And, again, we hear the whisper. But, it is usually too faint, too far away. And again, we wonder.

*Remembering Your Destiny* does not necessarily mean arriving at an end point. It is an ongoing, lifelong process. Each of the Twelve Practices outlined in this book plays a part in this process. Some of the practices will help you to remember in subtle ways. Other exercises will bring more obvious results.

If you come across an idea or practice in the book that you cannot accept, just leave it and continue on. I have read several books that contain ideas I found beyond my willingness to accept, yet within many of the same publications I have also found life-changing ideas. We all must be critical of what we read or hear and select only those tenets which are in congruence with our deepest values and integrity.

The best way to work with uncovering your destiny is to dedicate a notebook to it. At first I used a wire-bound notebook, but later switched to a ring binder, so I could insert new materials and move others. It has served me well. You may also wish to have on hand a portable timer. Many of the exercises are designed to last two or three minutes, others ten minutes. Some people are helped by timing these at first to get an idea of how long two minutes is. (It can surprise you.)

If you wish, you may order *The Destiny Process Workbook*. Write to the address at the back of this book for more information. The workbook contains the exercises and worksheets in a format to fit into a three-ring notebook.

Spend time with each practice until you are comfortable with it. You may find (as did I) that you will return to certain exercises from time to time. In fact, after each Initiation (see Chapter 12), you may find yourself beginning again with Access and using the new insights you receive to further develop your Master Destiny Statement.

Although Access seems logical for the first practice and Initiation seems to fall as the last one, you may find yourself drawn to one of the other practices. The order is not as important as your developing each skill. Each practice is like a part of a spider web. When you touch one, the others move. As you develop skill in all of them, the entire structure becomes stronger. The ones you are already good at may be the ones you want to work at the most. However, becoming proficient in the full range will make your experience that much richer.

After mastering each practice at one level and feeling confident with each, you may find that you are now ready to develop them at ever higher levels. So far as I know, we never get "there" but continue to grow eternally.

## *Annotated List of the Twelve Practices*

*Access:* Tapping into the ethers; the collective unconscious. Everything you want or need to know is already in existence. There is nothing new — perhaps elements rearranged in ways that are unfamiliar to you at this time, but it's all there. Gaining Access to this information is a matter of building and practicing skills.

*Articulation:* The ability to express clearly and precisely. Words and the emotions behind them have great power. The sharper our ability to exhibit this practice, the sharper our results will be.

*Intention:* The inner drive and commitment with which you carry out your plans. Practicing Intention gives you the strength to stick to living the way you want to.

*Visioning:* Bringing all our senses to bear on a desired event or result. This includes seeing, feeling, smelling, touching, tasting and experiencing it.

*Projection:* Although there is only one Creator, we have the power to work with the creative energy in forming that which is necessary and desired to complete our destiny. This is the same energy with which Jesus worked. He told us we could do even more with it.

**Allowance:** We block much of our good by erecting walls or by getting caught up in the struggle or drama of life. When we practice Allowance, we give ourselves permission for our good to enter in.

**Focus:** If we bring a single-mindedness to a subject, we increase many fold its likelihood of accomplishment. The practice of Focus brings about more in a shorter time.

**Forgiveness:** We forgive a situation or person by removing our negative energy from it. This frees us from the inhibiting energy that was draining us. Forgiveness does not imply agreement. Instead, it defines a healthy approach for facing and dealing with difficult situations and people.

**Discipline:** Just as a pianist must practice daily, we must develop a consistent approach not only to the Practices, but to our entire life as well. Discipline does not mean rigidity, but it often does mean giving up a short-term pleasure for long-term fulfillment.

**Congruence:** Most of us live incongruently in one or more areas. This conflict between our professed beliefs and our outpicturing can block our good. When we live congruently, we do not spend energy trying to resolve the conflict. Living congruently opens up channels to our good.

**World Service:** We must all be responsible for our life in its fullest manifestation. This includes being of service to others and finding our right livelihood. World Service may or may not have to do with your vocation, but it *does* show up in how you conduct yourself in your vocation.

**Initiation:** Going through various, well-defined steps as you grow. Each person's experiences are unique, yet they all have elements in common. As we grow in the Twelve

Practices, we will experience more and more Initiations, allowing us to manifest at higher and higher levels.

❧ ❧ ❧

We must be proficient in all Twelve Practices to live fully and manifest completely the destiny we were sent here to experience. There is no specific order in which to learn and become proficient in the Practices, as they all tie together.

In addition, as you become accomplished in a Practice, you will learn new ways to experience it. Each Practice carries with it practical applications in our lives. You will find that, as you begin to adopt the Practices as a part of your life, you will develop your own exercises and your own methods of progressing through your destiny.

*Chapter 1*

*Access*

Have you ever puzzled over something or tried to think of a new approach to a problem or a healthy way to resolve a ticklish situation? In doing so, has the answer eluded you for a time, but then, in a flash, the answer burst forth? Or have you ever uttered something extremely profound and found yourself wondering, "Where did *that* come from?"

Some famous (and not so famous) people have found their answers in dreams or dreamlike states. Robert Louis Stevenson claimed he could turn his desires over to his "brownies," or magical helpers, and at night they would help him write his stories. Buckminster Fuller, seeking the answer to a particular problem, didn't speak for a year as he searched within for the answer. It came.

Thomas Edison took cat naps standing up, his arm outstretched, an object in his hand. He would ponder the question on his mind. When he dozed off, his hand would fall, dropping the object, awakening him. Often, at that moment, the answer would flash in front of him.

These extraordinary people took advantage of what many of us "regular folks" now know: the answers we seek, the knowledge we crave are already available. It's no coincidence that the telephone, automobile, light bulb and many of our modern conveniences were developed in more than one place simultaneously, without the inventors knowing each other.

The first practice, Access, is concerned with helping you to take the first step in gaining entry into tapping into the source of this knowledge. You can get to the point where you quite literally hear the voice of God. This may come in several forms, such as dreams, visions, certain precise feelings, and, of course, a voice. You will learn to discern these messages from the usual chatter and clatter that goes on in most of our minds. It has a distinct character, but it is different for each individual. That is why it is so important for you to practice the exercises, to question the results and to experiment until you recognize it unmistakably. The more you practice, the more proficient you become at recognizing it. The better you get at recognizing it, the more the universe will open up to you.

The modern prophet, Charles Fillmore, used the term "ether" to describe the source. Most people I've talked with who display an enormous capacity to tap into this ether have told me that they practice almost every day to maintain their ability to use the skill.

Access goes beyond simple intuition in that it is more precise and more recognizable than the occasional hunch we get. Hunches are actually a facet of Access, yet, through developing the skill of Access, you can learn to recognize and regularly tap into that which you have taken advantage of only occasionally. You will learn to discriminate what is useful and what is not. You will usually be able to tell what is mere vanity and what is pushing you toward realizing your destiny.

The two main skills in this practice are:
- knowing what to ask
- understanding what you receive

I used to think it was important to know the answers. Now, it seems that knowing which question to ask is more important. I've learned that the answers are ready for plucking. However, finding the tree on which they're growing can often be a challenge.

As you travel through this book, you will learn many ways of receiving information that will contribute to living your destiny. In this chapter we'll cover some basic skills and a little philosophy.

As a young woman, I was struggling to finish college. Divorced and with a small child, I wanted to create the best life possible for us. My first step was finishing college. During summer break, I was visiting my parents for a few days. One morning I woke up with a strong feeling (almost to the point of hearing a voice inside me) that I should return to the college town where I was living.

I had begun to understand the wisdom of following some of these "hunches" and decided to follow my feelings and left that morning. Less than an hour after I arrived home, I received a phone call from the college library, asking if I would like to work there until I graduated. I had been hoping for this job as it answered many of my needs.

Later, I asked the person who hired me what she would have done had she not reached me. (This was in the era before answering machines.) She replied, "Oh, I would have called the next name on our list."

Had I known what was happening at the time, I would have cultivated the skill of Access much more highly at an earlier age. Fortunately, I paid attention enough times to get me through some rough times in the years to follow.

Why is it important to develop the skill of Access? I hope the answer is obvious. Within the ether that Charles Fillmore described is all we need to know to rediscover why we're here, what our mission is, and how to go about bringing its reality into our lives. Some people call this the voice of God or the Holy Spirit. I just call it Spirit for simplicity's sake. I figure God knows what I mean.

As far as I can tell, listening for, learning to recognize and then applying what we receive is pretty much a lifetime project. Just when I think I have this Access thing down perfectly, I am exposed to new levels and a greater awareness of some aspect of life. Sometimes I am forced to take a new look at myself. Other times I realize how foolish I've just been. And, every once in a while, I get to see something wonderful and profound that increases my sense of wonder and awe at the magnificence of it all.

A few years ago, my husband was about to take a dramatic step in business. Although I agreed with the action, I got a message that the timing was wrong and that he should delay the move. I dug my heels in and said we needed to wait. This is rather unusual in our household, as he is very wise and almost always makes appropriate decisions. After many lively discussions, he reluctantly agreed. In a little more than a year, some unanticipated events occurred which made the action not only appropriate, but lucrative as well.

This was a big risk for me, because I was not told why we should wait, only that the action shouldn't be taken for at least a year. But, the feeling was so strong and the message so clear that I followed it and it made all the difference.

What continues to amaze me is the ease with which we can Access this knowledge. It is always present, always at hand. It is never *not* here. It is as close as your willingness to listen and to get out of the way of whatever is blocking it. Sometimes, as in the example above, it takes some courage to follow the voice. You can build courage by beginning with small things, such as asking which way to turn at a light or which outfit to wear to work. Soon you will discern what the voice of Spirit sounds like.

You might have heard the story of the sculptor who, when asked how he knew what to carve in that big block of marble, he answered, "I just begin carving and chip away anything that doesn't look like the statue."

This is what we must do in gaining Access to the wisdom of the universe. We must learn to quit listening to the noise that is not like Spirit and begin to recognize that which *is* like Spirit. How do we learn to recognize it? Practice, my child, practice.

When I was first applying this skill many years ago, I decided to test it and asked for directions to a certain place. I received strong hunches to turn at certain places and, after about ten minutes, ended up right back where I started. "What was that all about?" I asked. "Just wanted to see if you would follow directions," came the reply. I was then guided to exactly the place I wanted to be. (My Spirit has a healthy sense of humor.)

You may think Access is the most valuable in the big, dramatic events of life. While the application of this skill has certainly saved me from disaster, I find its utilization most helpful in the small, almost mundane areas of my life.

For instance, I recently reached for a bottle of my favorite juice. As I did so, I was guided to buy another variety. Shortly thereafter, many people became seriously ill from drinking juice from the brand I rejected. The incident was so widespread it made the national news. I gratefully thanked Spirit for the advice.

Not long after that I was ready to sign up to run in a fun run. I had looked forward to this event for some time and was curious about the reluctance I was feeling about signing up. Finally, I decided I would register on the day of the race, even though that's not my usual habit. I awoke that morning to find a blanket of snow on the ground.

These are little things and yet paying attention as much as possible to the voice of Spirit makes my life run so much more smoothly. Many of the little trials that disrupt my life are avoided simply because I tune in. My husband and I make a regular practice of asking what Spirit is saying to us.

Throughout this book, many of the exercises you learn will increase your ability to Access, so you will find this chapter woven into other sections of the book. The Twelve Practices can't be separated any more than you can separate your breath from your lungs. Learning is all interconnected. The more you practice and become skilled in one area, the more it will contribute to the others.

In some of the exercises in the book, I ask you to become quiet. Rather than repeat in each one how to become relaxed, I'll outline the quick, easy method I use to still my mind and body. This is not the same as deep meditation. In fact, once you become skilled at quieting yourself, you can do it in a moment just by deciding to do so, almost without conscious thought. (This comes in handy at stoplights and during stressful meetings.) If you already practice a method of becoming quiet that works for you, please use it as you wish.

## *Exercise 1:*
### *How To Become Quiet*

- Get into a position that is comfortable for you, either sitting or reclining.
- Take a deep breath. Exhale forcefully through your mouth. As you exhale, relax your body.
- Beginning at your toes and moving quickly up through the top of your head, consciously think of relaxing. (In some systems, the practitioners ask you to stop at each muscle group

and tighten and relax it. That really isn't necessary for these exercises, but, if you're having a lot of trouble relaxing you might wish to try it.)

- Take another deep breath and again exhale forcefully. Shift any areas of your body that still feel tense.
- Take a slow, deep breath and exhale slowly through the nasal passages. You should now be relaxed enough to complete the exercises in which you are to become quiet.

## *Exercise 2:*
### *Building the Skill*

Become quiet. For two minutes do nothing but concentrate on your ears. Do not consciously listen for anything. As you practice this daily, you may begin to hear faint sounds. You might become aware of sounds around you that you never heard before. Some people have reported hearing chords or definite music. Others have told me that their overall hearing improved just by doing this exercise. Keep a record in your Destiny Notebook about your experiences.

You may find that, after a few weeks of practice, you begin to pick up messages you never heard before. I'm not suggesting that you will begin to hear strange voices, but you may sense that you are receiving information that is new to you or "hunches" about a direction to take. Begin to pay attention to this, following it if you wish to test it.

Keep in mind the following four points if you are ever uncertain about whether the information you are receiving is appropriate:

- You will never be asked to do anything that would harm another.
- You will not be directed to engage in dishonest behavior or to do that which is of low character.
- You will not be asked to do that which will harm you in the long run. (Sometimes, when adjustments are being made you may wonder about this one.)
- Any information you receive that is truly from your higher self will be for the highest good of all concerned. DO NOT follow intuition that intimates anything harmful.

ぷ   ぷ   ぷ

I now use this skill for everything from finding parking places, to consulting with individual clients, to cooking. I know that the direction I need, no matter what, will be there if I am willing to listen, to Access and to follow.

## *How to Use the Practice of Access to Remember Your Destiny.*

In order to begin the process of uncovering your destiny, you must understand the range of your gifts and talents. We all have hundreds, perhaps thousands, of these abilities, some seemingly unremarkable, others outstanding. Many of these capabilities we are not even aware of, yet they all contribute to help us fulfill our role.

As I have said before, we were seeded with what we need to carry out our purpose. It does not, however, mean that we were born fully able to express these abilities. Some of them must be developed and used in order to come to full flower.

But, first, you must know what they are. This is the first step in the Destiny Process. Understanding this aspect of your creation is the seed for your full expression. Most people are surprised by the volume of gifts that begins to pour out once they start this process. Others find they can't seem to break through to anything. This may be due to years of input from themselves or others which has convinced them that they don't have much to offer.

If the latter sounds like you, I'm giving you notice right now. *You are a gifted, talented person.* Don't ever believe anyone who says otherwise. Even the simplest of talents can be an important part of your destiny.

The following exercise will help you unlock and recognize your gifts. Read it through before you engage yourself in it. The first time you experience it, you may wish to read a section, then relax into it. After you have practiced it a few times, you will be able to complete it without reading. For your convenience and enjoyment, this meditation is also available on tape with lovely background music.

This is **Step One**. You will find the rest of the steps described after the meditation.

[Note: If you become uncomfortable or uneasy at any point in any of the meditations, open your eyes, take a deep breath and stop the process. Do not continue if you do not feel it is in your best interest. If you are under the care of a mental health professional, please consult with that individual before beginning.]

## Meditation 1:
## Unlocking The Seed

To unlock for the seed of your destiny:

Close your eyes. Become quiet. Rest in that quiet space for a few minutes, listening to your breathing. Feel yourself becoming lighter and lighter. See yourself in a room with soft lights and a high ceiling. Before you is an archway marked "Tunnel of Destiny." You feel a magnetic pull toward this tunnel. You see that it is a beautiful place, filled with soft, multi-colored lights. You hear relaxing music coming from within as it beckons you to enter.

As you approach the entrance to the tunnel, you see a radiant being, bathed in light guarding the passage. This is the Gatekeeper. You feel very safe with this being and you know it is there to support you and guide you.

"What do you want," asks the Gatekeeper softly and lovingly.

"I want to find my destiny," you respond.

"Is this what you truly want?" asks the Gatekeeper.

Carefully consider your answer to the question. When you are ready to enter the tunnel and seek your destiny, respond by saying, "I am ready." If you feel uncomfortable about proceeding, take a deep breath, open your eyes and stop the meditation. You may return to it later.

The Gatekeeper stands aside and allows you to pass. You step inside the tunnel, still feeling safe and protected. As you relax even more, you find yourself gently pulled forward into the tunnel.

As you move deeper into the tunnel, voices begin to penetrate your mind, mixing and blending in a celestial harmony. The chorus grows more loving and powerful as voices are added. You recognize it as the sound of universal love.

The sound surrounds you and begins to penetrate your cells, even to the DNA level. As the sound fills you, you feel yourself beginning to vibrate to the rhythm of the chanting, surrendering to its magical harmonies and letting go of any earthly worries.

As you relax even more, you feel yourself becoming lighter and lighter as you start to blend with the lights and sounds. As you move along, you notice that you are taking on the characteristics of this heavenly experience.

As you near the end of the tunnel, you realize that you have left your earthly body behind and are now transformed into your spirit body. As you emerge from the tunnel, you find yourself in a large, beautiful room, filled with soft light and plush surroundings. This is the Hall of Gifts. You are approached by a loving, kindly being who tells you that you will now learn about the gifts and talents with which you were seeded in order to carry out your destiny. As you listen, the being tells you about and shows you the many gifts you were given.

Listen until the being is finished, knowing you will remember all you were told. When you feel the session is complete, re-enter the tunnel and return to the start.

ช   ช   ช

When you have finished the Inner Work, spend a few minutes recording what you saw and experienced, either in your journal or on a tape, even if you didn't understand what you were told.

If you saw nothing or can remember nothing, list any talents or gifts you think you might possess. At some level, you know them already. This exercise merely helps you to access that knowledge.

ช   ช   ช

Do this exercise for at least three days, listing as many gifts as you can, even if you find yourself repeating some. This is no time to be modest or self-deprecating. You don't have to show your list to anyone. Many years ago, when this exercise was first revealed to me, I was actually embarrassed to write down some of the gifts I was shown in the meditation. And I was alone in the room! So, put that concern aside and just write.

Keep these sheets in your Destiny Notebook.

*Step Two:* For three days make lists of things you like or want to do. At the end of those three days highlight or circle ten to twenty items that appeal the most to you.

*Step Three:* Begin to notice patterns within steps one and two. Do any of them go together? You will often find yourself being drawn to those things for which you have some ability.

For instance, if you like to pick flowers and arrange them, one of your gifts may be appreciation of beauty.

*Step Four:* Begin to link the matches in step three with what it might mean as far as understanding your destiny. In the above example, a part of your destiny might be to create beauty in the world.

When I began this quest so many years ago, I was fortunate enough to be vacationing in Hawaii. I had set a goal to understand why I was put on this earth by the time I left the islands. Every morning for two weeks I arose at five. (You call this a vacation?) With a notebook in hand I sat on the balcony which overlooked the ocean. I went through the meditation you just read which had recently been shown to me by Spirit and performed the four steps.

By the end of that time, I knew that my destiny had something to do with helping others see their greatness and developing the tools and means for them to use their greatness to help create a heaven on earth. What I knew about my destiny was still pretty formless, but I had discovered the germ. Since that time, I have been growing and developing that embryo. I figured out early in this process that, as I grew, new layers of this destiny would be revealed to me and, like everyone, I am still in this process of growing and developing. That's half the fun: we never actually "get there." We simply continue to peel away layers and experience new levels of growth and discovery.

We will discuss further steps in the Destiny Process as we get further into the practices.

ଝ   ଝ   ଝ

While we're discussing Access, let's look at some practical ways to utilize it. I've already told you about how it helped me while I was in college. Here are a couple of other ways it has helped me and others to save time, money and well-being.

One day, upon arriving at the grocery store, I discovered I had forgotten my check book. I had eight dollars in my purse, not enough to buy even two thirds of what was on my list. Because I know that God is very practical and helps me even in the most mundane of situations, I said, "God, you know what is on my grocery list and how much money I have. How about it?" God said, "You can get everything but the pine nuts." (We often have these sorts of conversations. Fortunately, neither of us speaks out loud, so I still fit into polite society.)

Sure enough, Spirit led me to everything I needed and guided me as to what quantities to buy. And, almost everything was on sale or some kind of close out. The cashier rang up $7.89. All that and I had 11 cents left over!

A friend of mine who has no sense of direction whatsoever was lost in a suburb of Seattle. She was alone and it was getting dark. So she pulled over to the curb and got quiet for a few moments, asking to be led back to the freeway. Startled, she heard a voice saying, "If I led Moses out of the wilderness, don't you think I can get you out of Burien?"

She began to drive, receiving very strong messages about where to turn. In three minutes she was back on the freeway.

Recently, while driving home one night on a rural road, Spirit warned me loudly and abruptly, "An animal is about to cross in front of your car." I quickly prayed that I be harmless to all I encounter and became very alert. I knew this was an extraordinary event, as the adrenaline was rushing through my body, keeping me alert. I drive this road almost every day and nothing like this had ever happened. So I paid attention. Sure enough, about 30 seconds later, a cat suddenly darted out in front of me. Because I listened, my senses were heightened, and I was able to stop in time. If I had not heeded the warning, I would have hit the cat, causing me and its owner much trauma. It wouldn't have done the cat any good, either.

To be able to use Access on a daily, practical basis, you must practice. Practice following your hunches on minor things, such as whom to call for a particular piece of information or as a sales call. You might see if you can correctly identify who is calling you when the phone rings or who has written to you before you pull the mail out of the box. Before you look at your watch, guess the exact time and see how close you come. These are simple exercises, yet you would be surprised at how well they can build your skill of Access if you practice them daily.

For simple yes or no questions, I now recognize a subtle physical reaction in my head that gives me immediate feedback. The body has an intelligence of its own and can tell us far more than we think. For that reason, I often use a pendulum to help me gain the answers I need. It's also a lot of fun.

## *Using a Pendulum for Access*

A pendulum can be a useful device for tapping into the wisdom inherent in your body. Although it seems a little "woo-woo," it really isn't. In fact, it's pretty mechanical in how it operates.

When you use a pendulum, you are asking questions to which, somewhere inside of you, you have the answer. If you have properly set up your responses, it is then just a matter of asking the right questions, getting out of the way, and seeing the answers. Most people use a pendulum to get "Yes" or "No" answers in an easy and fun manner.

Your body and inner self contain an incredible amount of wisdom. Your subconscious picks up everything that you have ever experienced and stores it. Each cell of your body has its own intelligence. Your higher self is in touch with God at all times, even though you're not always aware of it. As we've progressed through life, the "wiring" that has connected our body and higher self to our conscious awareness has sort of rusted. Using a pendulum can help to dissolve the rust and reconnect you to these parts of yourself.

The pendulum itself has no power. It's merely an instrument, such as a pen. It's the operator (you) who creates the outcome. I was first exposed to this concept when I was a small child. My grandfather taught me to dowse, using a stick in the shape of a "Y" to locate water under the ground. At that age, the skill came naturally, as I had no preconceived notions to keep me from feeling the pull of the forked stick when it was over water. When, as an adult, I was exposed to the pendulum, it practically leapt out of my hand when I asked the first question.

Many of the people I teach how to use the pendulum do not have immediate results, but, if they practice a little, they are able to work with it quite well. One of my colleagues, who is an excellent dowser, has rarely seen her pendulum move more than a half inch in any direction, yet she uses it very effectively. So, don't be concerned about your first efforts. Some people who had absolutely no results at first have become the most skilled pendulum users.

What is a pendulum? It's simply an object that can swing easily from a chain or string. I've seen some exotic carved or gemstone pendulums with gold chains as well as an old bead tied to a string. I've used pendant necklaces, a small microphone at the end of a cord, and a Christmas ornament on a string. It's all the same.

To work with a pendulum, hold the chain or string between your fingers and let the object at the end dangle. When you ask a question, the pendulum moves in a pre-determined direction to tell you yes, no, maybe or neutral (or whatever else you've set up) so you can receive an answer.

The pendulum moves through what is called an ideo-motor response. This means that tiny muscles in your fingers move almost imperceptibly to cause the chain and then the pendulum to move in the direction of the answer. To use a pendulum properly and receive correct information, some conditions must be met:

1. If you want to get the best answer, you must be neutral. In other words, if you have an emotional stake in the answer, you should probably ask someone else to use the pendulum for you. For instance, if you have just interviewed for a job and want it badly, this may not be a good subject for your pendulum activities. Otherwise your answer *may* be skewed. Before asking any questions, I always ask, "Am I neutral about this?" If I get a "No" response," I do one of three things, depending on the urgency of the answer (see #2 under Procedure for Using the Pendulum).

2. You must become a good questioner. Your answers often reflect the quality and clarity of your questions. Questions are usually those which can be answered "Yes" or "No," although throughout this book, I will give examples of other ways to use the pendulum to Access your body's wisdom. If you are getting noncommittal or strange answers,

re-visit your question. When I'm asking questions, I take a moment to become still, then I concentrate on the question(s) at hand so my entire being is Focused. At that point I generally get the clearest answers.

3. You must be in a position to trust yourself and your body. If you are completely out of touch with any inner wisdom or are a person who doesn't trust this sort of approach, using a pendulum will probably not be your best form of Access — at least not at first. It may require much more work on your part if you want to use this method of Access. Trust is the key ingredient.


A good example of staying neutral occurred during one of my seminars. When my son and daughter-in-law were expecting a baby, for some reason at the beginning, my son and I thought it might be a girl. I fixed that in my mind and, in prayer, generally pictured the baby as a girl. However, at a demonstration of using the pendulum, I did an experiment, asking the audience to see if they could determine whether the baby was to be a boy or a girl. The results were split 50-50. (I did not announce what I thought.) When I used my pendulum, it said the baby was a girl. Alexander, my darling grand*son* proved to me the wisdom of being neutral before I ask a question.

## *Procedure for Using the Pendulum*

1. When you begin to practice with the pendulum, hold the chain lightly between your thumb and forefinger. Ask, "Show me which direction is 'Yes.'" The pendulum will probably swing either horizontally or vertically from your body.

   At first, it may seem as if the pendulum is not moving at all. If you receive no response, be patient. Tell yourself that you really wish to use this method of Access to help you live a better life and gain insight into various happenings. Don't worry if it moves only slightly.

   It's best to start when you are quiet and undisturbed. This ensures that you can take some time and not feel rushed to get results right away.

   After you have determined which direction is "Yes," ask which way is "No." Although for most people the pendulum moves at right angles, I have seen examples of it moving on the diagonal or in a circle. For me "Yes" is at a 90 degree angle from my body, and "No" is parallel. When something is being worked on (e.g. getting me to neutral), the pendulum moves in a clockwise direction. If the question is too vague or the answer is neutral, it moves in a counter-clockwise direction.

2.  Holding the chain lightly, ask, "Am I in a neutral place?" If the answer is "Yes," proceed with your questions. If "No," I usually just ask Spirit, "Get me to neutral." The pendulum circles around and stops. I then ask again. If the response is still, "No," I go on to something else or call up a trusted friend to ask the question for me.

3.  Once you have established the answer criteria and determined that you are neutral about the answers, decide on some questions. If you've never worked with a pendulum before, ask some obvious questions like, "Is my name Fred?", or "Am I 35 years old?" Anything that can be answered easily with "Yes" or "No."

    As you get proficient at interpreting the answers to the obvious questions, move into questions that are more complex. You might ask questions such as, "What should I wear to work?" or "Which format would be better for this presentation?" Your pendulum will swing to "Yes" when it is over the preferred choice. Remember you already know this information at some level. Using the pendulum simply helps you to Access the knowledge quickly and easily.

4. When you ask questions, Focus on the question and your desire to know the truth. If you are distracted and unfocused you will probably receive answers which reflect that.

*Caution:* As with anything of this sort, it is easy to become dependent upon the pendulum. Remember that it has no power in and of itself. You must still use your wisdom to interpret and act upon the answers. Common sense has never gone out of style, nor has the use of accumulated knowledge and good research. Always act in the highest manner possible if you wish to manifest your destiny.

*Chapter 2*

# *Articulation*

If you have practiced the Access exercises, you may very well be getting an idea about your destiny. When I first started on my Destiny Process, I found myself in a sort of "round-robin" of getting flashes of ideas, writing them down, drafting some type of destiny statement, then starting again with the ideas. I found that the more clearly and precisely I was able to state what I understood about my destiny to that point, the more quickly it unfolded in my life — occasionally to my short-term chagrin and long-term gratitude.

To the extent that you are able to precisely and clearly express your destiny, the faster and more precisely it will unfold for you. It is now fairly common knowledge that much of our experience comes from the words we say, think or write. We live in a responsive universe that is constantly reshaping itself.

We must take care of what we create with our words. Not too long ago, my life seemed to be in constant turmoil, mostly because the events around me were interfering with my carefully orchestrated plans

I found myself saying, "I just don't have enough time. Nothing is going smoothly. Every time I make a plan, something interferes." In fact, the more I said that, the more it seemed to happen. After about three weeks of my life becoming increasingly frustrating, I realized what I had been saying. I then said, instead, "I now want my life to run smoothly. I have time for everything." I immediately felt an energy shift and became calm. The interesting part was that the events didn't change measurably for a few days; however, my approach to them did because I had changed my internal dialogue. And, of course, after I let go of the drama and began changing my words, the events of my life fit together perfectly.

On another occasion, I found myself using the phrase, "It just took my breath away," to describe wonderful scenes or happenings in my life, of which there were quite a few. Within about a week of adding this phrase to my lexicon, I noticed I was having some trouble breathing. Fortunately, I made the connection and quit using the phrase. The breathing difficulty left instantly.

I once read that every word we think and speak is a prayer. Look at your words and ask yourself, "What am I praying for?" If you don't like the answer, change your words.

A current phrase to describe something exquisite is to describe it as "to die for." Several of my friends and I were, in fact, using it, when we realized what we were saying. We now say a thing is "to live for."

Although, like all the practices, Articulation is a lifetime project, I find that, more and more, I'm catching myself when I use damaging words. When that happens, I say, aloud or mentally, "Change that." I then substitute a more positive phrase or word.

An old trick used by behavioral psychologists is to wear a rubber band around your wrist. When you find yourself thinking or speaking in the old way, snap the band. This slight sting reminds you not to say that again and to replace it with something more uplifting. This kind of therapy doesn't take long to kick in.

## *Exercise 3:*
### *Eliminating Damaging Phrases*

During the next week become acutely aware of not only how you are speaking, but how those around you use damaging phrases. You may find that it has become epidemic.

Keep a log and, as you proceed through your day, jot down any damaging phrases or words you hear or say. At the end of each day, change each word or phrase into a positive — or at least neutral — expression. This will help you not only to notice more acutely when it's happening, but it will give you a repertoire of phrases to substitute when you are tempted to use damaging language.

In the Bible it says, "Thou shalt also decree a thing, and it shall be established unto thee: and the light shall shine upon thy ways." Job 22:28

This means that, not only can your words afflict you, but they can uplift and change circumstances to your betterment as well.

Since every word we utter is a prayer, we can be creative in their use. In the Bible, Jesus didn't mumble when he wanted Lazarus to rise from the dead. He spoke firmly and clearly.

In one town I was driving around lost. I needed to make a phone call and finally found a pay phone. Although I was trying to listen, it didn't seem to be working. I was exhausted, frustrated and had virtually no patience left, when I discovered I had only a dime and paper money. Looking heavenward, I said (strongly), "God, I need a quarter and I need it now!" I don't usually make such demands, but, after all, it seemed to work for Jesus.

Not one second later I heard, "Kaching." I looked in the coin return and, sure enough, there was a quarter. I made the call, found my destination, and praised God's creative power all the while.

As you can see, I Articulated the need clearly and precisely and it was met.

So, what does this have to do with remembering your destiny? As you grow and develop in your destiny, you must learn to clearly and precisely define exactly what you want. This goes not just for your destiny, but for your goals, Intentions and anything else in your life.

One way Articulation is used to help you remember your destiny is the development of a destiny statement.

In the last chapter I told you how I used some vacation time to discover the foundation for understanding my destiny. By getting some insight into my gifts and talents and by looking at my preferred activities, I discovered that the root theme of it all was that I enjoyed helping others discover their own greatness. I also realized that, if an activity wasn't practical in some way, I would lose interest quickly. (I consider adding beauty, love, and fun to be very practical. You may differ with me here.)

My interest in helping others did not relate to the psychological or health areas, but to the application of truths in their lives. After working with articulating what I thought my destiny was, I came up with the following initial Destiny Statement:

> *"I am here to help others see their own greatness and to develop tools to help them create joy in their lives, and to be a part in making this a heaven on earth."*

Although this statement wasn't exactly elegant, it *did* express as much as I knew at the time about my destiny. And knowing this, I began the phase of my earthly journey that involved making more and more decisions based on this one statement. And, to paraphrase Robert Frost, "it has made all the difference."

Over the years, I have refined and sharpened this statement to the point where I now simply refer to my own destiny as "Toolbringer."

Many students I have talked to have said, "Well, I think I have an idea about my destiny, but I just can't put it into words." This may be so, but if you can't express it clearly in words or symbols, you probably will not express it in your outer world.

To begin the articulation of your destiny, follow this procedure. Use the same instructions for the relaxation exercise as in the chapter on Access. (All the relaxation exercises in this book are available on tape.)

## *Meditation 2:*
### *Articulating Your Destiny*

Relax and become quiet. You are once again at the entrance to the tunnel. The Gatekeeper tells you that this time you will be looking at the original blueprint from which you were fashioned.

"Are you ready to enter?" asks the Gatekeeper.

Again, consider your answer carefully, and when you are prepared, answer, "I am ready."

The music once again fills you as you travel through the beautiful tunnel. You feel more and more relaxed and filled with love and peace. When you exit, you find yourself in a large hall, filled with many beings just like you.

This section of the Hall is labeled "Blueprints." This is where your original blueprint is stored — the one your spirit self was created from. The Guardian of the Blueprints asks you what records you want to see.

The Guardian silently motions for you to follow. You are led to a beautiful place where you may sit comfortably or stand.

The Guardian brings you your blueprint. It is printed on a parchment of pure light and the lines sparkle like precious iridescent jewels. You may inspect it, remembering all you see. Take as much time as you wish. Your blueprint may reveal even more of your gifts and talents. You may wish to gain a deeper understanding of the meaning and use of a particular latent talent you possess.

When you have finished reviewing your blueprint, the Guardian brings you another parchment. As you unroll it and look at it it, words begin to form. These words are clues to your destiny. As the first word forms, it lifts off the page and flows into your heart. Feel the essence of this word as it takes up residence and fills you with its wonder. As each succeeding word forms, it, too, fills your being. And you remember all you experience.

After the last word forms and fills you, the Guardian escorts you back to the entrance to the tunnel, inviting you to return whenever you wish. You slowly return to the room in which you began the meditation. Take a deep breath, stretch, and open your eyes.

***Step One:*** Immediately write down everything you remember about this meditation. If you saw nothing or can remember nothing, spend a few minutes writing about what you think the Guardian of the Blueprints looks like and what the Hall of Blueprints looks like. You might even fantasize about what might be written on the parchments.

***Step Two:*** Repeat this meditation once or twice a day for at least three days. I suggest using the exercise until you feel a sense of closure with it. Each time you complete it, write down everything you remember.

***Step Three:*** Examine the lists you made while practicing Access as well as the writings you have just done. Look for patterns.

***Step Four:*** Using all the above, plus your intuition, write a preliminary Destiny Statement, such as the one I began with. Continue to work with this statement for the next few weeks.

ꝋ  ꝋ  ꝋ

In the networking classes I teach throughout the country, I ask the participants to describe *exactly* the type of person they would like to meet. I hear amazing stories from these people about the coincidences that occur when they are able to articulate exactly what they are looking for. Often, when these descriptions are shared in class, another person in the room will say, "Why, I know someone exactly like that!" Arrangements are then made to link the two.

## *Asking for What You Want.*

In James 4:2-3, we are given two reasons why we don't get what we want in life. The first reason is that we simply don't ask. *"Ye have not because ye ask not."*

The author here is not referring to those wimpy little wishful hopes that spring with a sigh from our lips or remain hidden inside a fortress of fear. Neither is he referring to begging. He is talking about clear, bold, precise requests, with the conviction that something will happen, but the maturity to deal with the outcome.

The second indictment of our approach is that, even if we do get around to asking, we don't ask properly. We ask only for those things which will satisfy our momentary whims. *"Ye ask, and receive not, because ye ask amiss, that ye may consume it upon your lusts."* The author is not admonishing us for having possessions, but for pinning our hopes and dreams upon them and not seeing the larger picture. When we speak precisely from a clear mind and a pure heart, that is very different.

He goes on to call us adulterers and adulteresses. He is not talking about crossing the sanctity of the marriage vows, although I'm sure he wasn't in favor of that. He is telling us that we adulterate, or pollute, our thinking and, therefore, the outcome is equally polluted.

We adulterate our words by speaking of lack and telling people how awful it is. If you think of each word as a prayer, consider carefully what you are praying for. It can be difficult to stay pure, especially when those around us are pointing out "realities." While we need to understand fully the situations around us, we can still speak words of hope and of solutions rather than those of hate, division and problems.

## *Articulate Self-expression.*

Sometimes we confuse expressing our point of view with not needing to defend it. If you still feel you need to defend your point of view, yet you suppress and stuff that need, you're not addressing the issue inside that needs your attention. In fact, you're probably making it worse as you suffer in the silence.

A colleague of mine who is high-minded woke up one morning and found that her voice had fled somewhere in the night. After treating herself and getting no relief, she made herself quiet and asked if there was a reason for it. Immediately she realized that she needed to be open and up front about a work situation. She had wanted tell her boss that she was no longer willing to be the object of his uncontrolled anger, but was reluctant to speak up. My colleague also realized that she had to be free of anger herself (see the chapter on Forgiveness). She was then able to tell her truth without making the boss appear wrong. Not only did the situation reverse itself, but her throat cleared up within just a few hours.

Perhaps, when you feel you need to defend your point of view, you're afraid of some sort of loss. The need to be right generally comes from this base of fear. So does the need to be heard, understood and agreed with.

A woman called me for consulting once. She was upset with her husband because, in her opinion, he didn't listen to her. At first, I thought she wanted to discuss how to make the relationship better, but it soon became clear that the objective of her call was something entirely different. She said, over and over, "I just want to be heard." What she really wanted was to get her way and for him to be wrong. After exploring the concept of telling her truth without making him wrong (and getting nowhere), I gently suggested that they seek marriage counseling. However, since there was "nothing wrong with her," she refused and went elsewhere to get support for her "rightness."

The desire to express a point of view is completely natural. It is part of our expression as humans. To the extent that we can simply state our point of view and let go of the attachment of being heard, understood and agreed with will say a lot about how mature and self-actualized we are. This does not mean we ignore situations where harm is being done. The ability to remain emotionally detached from a circumstance will help us to deal with it from a higher point of view.

Suppressing that which *needs* to be said by us can bring about unpleasant side effects, such as on-going abuse, resentment over situations, destruction of relationships, and general unhappiness. Gaining the courage to speak our truth without making the other person wrong can take some work. Try the following exercise to help you be more Articulate about your truth and still keep those relationships that are worth Preserving.

## Exercise 4:
## Telling Your Truth

Write answers to the following questions in your Destiny notebook:

1. What have you been resisting saying because of the reactions of someone else? This could be something you have not said before or something that shows a history of negative responses.

2. What frightens you or upsets you about the reactions, real or imagined? What might you lose?
3. What would you gain by telling your truth?
4. How could you state this without making anyone else wrong?

One approach to this is to write out a script, thinking of different ways the other person might react and ways you can respond. Read the chapter on Allowance to help you let go of any attachment to the other person's response.

*Chapter 3*

*Intention*

In my book, *The New Success,* I devoted an entire chapter to the role of Intention in developing a successful life. Since then I have learned even more about Intention and feel even more strongly that the practice of Intention is necessary to not only determine your destiny, but to develop the strength requisite to create its outpicturing.

Intention is the practice of determining in advance how you will think, act and speak no matter what the circumstances around you. It is, in essence, setting the quality and integrity with which you will live life.

It can be quite specific. You may decide before making a phone call that it is your Intention to speak your truth (such as saying "no" to something not in your best interest), even if the person on the other end of the line doesn't want to hear it.

It may be more general, such as choosing to live in order. When you set an Intention, then remember to remain in that consciousness, you "hold" an Intention.

We can build a life that is lived moment by moment, through Intention. For instance, before you get out of bed in the morning, let your thoughts roam to the kind of day you want to have. Ask yourself, "What is my Intention for this day?" Maybe you need to stay Focused on a project. Perhaps you want to remain calm in the face of adversity. Or, it could be your Intention to simply enjoy each moment.

Intention must be predetermined. That is, you must set your Intention before entering into a situation. It is often too difficult to decide on an Intention in the "heat of battle."

Think about Intention when you interact with your family or co-workers. In a heated discussion with your mate, you may hold the Intention to behave with the highest good for all concerned in mind. Or, you may set an Intention to not have to be right or to win, but to simply remain in love and peace. (Try that for a whole day!)

I am often asked about the difference between goals and Intention. While the two are closely related, there are some important differences. I encourage people to set goals; however, the goals themselves are meaningless unless driven by Intention.

The biggest difference between goals and Intentions is that goals are about where you're going. Intention is about where you're coming from internally.

Experts in goal-setting teach that a goal must be specific, measurable, attainable, and have a completion date.

An Intention, on the other hand:

- states how you wish to conduct yourself,
- indicates from which inner quality or principle your actions will originate, and
- acts as the force behind your achievements.

While goals need to be attainable, reaching our goals is not always under our complete control. For instance, if I were to run in a three-mile race, my goal might be to win first place. Winning, however, often depends on who else shows up. So, my goal is partially dependent upon me and partially dependent on whether a faster runner got up early that morning and came to the race with her own goal to win the gold.

In that same race I may set an Intention to do everything in my power to win or to do the best I can, following my own criteria for what that means. This Intention is always under my complete control. The Intention becomes my driving mechanism and winning then becomes my preference. Then, if I win, it's great; if I don't, I will be happy that I have done my very best.

Goals are outcome-oriented. Intention is process-oriented. If you are a goal-driven, outcome-oriented person and this works well for you, I don't recommend changing unless this behavior is causing you to lose sleep or behave in unhealthy ways.

You can judge for yourself if your system works by observing what happens to you when you don't achieve your goals. Does "failure" cause you anguish, anger or frustration, or do you simply keep plowing the ground and moving? If you cause yourself pain and lapse into despair, you may consider switching to a more Intention-oriented approach to your plans.

A benefit of Intention-oriented behavior is that, if you don't accomplish your goal (especially one that is not totally in your control), you won't be thrown as far off balance by it.

I remember an incident that happened when I had a real job. My boss and I were reviewing my work goals for the coming quarter. One of the goals he had assigned to me was to make sure that all the managers in our division attended a certain training class. After thinking for a minute, I asked him, "Would you agree that goals which are entirely under our control are generally the ones we should be measured against?" He replied in the affirmative.

"Well," I continued, "since these managers don't report directly to me, the best I can do is try to influence them and their bosses to attend this class. I can also program a database to track attendance and send out regular attendance reports."

To my boss' credit, he saw the truth of what I was saying. We rewrote the goal so that I would provide the reports and communicate the status of attendance.

This was a small thing, yet it could have affected my performance rating as well as my blood pressure. (By the way, all 1,000 managers *did* attend the training class. But I was not the one who had to cajole and persuade them. Their bosses were delegated that responsibility.)

Goals are about what you do. Intention is about who you are. The outcome of a goal and an Intention may be identical, but the energy behind the results is far different.

When we are working from Intention, the outcome of an event becomes a preference rather than a driving life force. Strangely enough, we often accomplish more when working from Intention because our energy is used more effectively and we are able to Focus on that which is at hand.

Are there times when goals are preferable to Intention? Absolutely. If we were caught inside a burning building, my goal would be to get out safely. I would be committed to the outcome. In life-threatening situations, an outcome-orientation may be far more favorable than simply preferring an outcome. At least it is for me.

However, for our normal day-to-day interactions, setting preferences rather than goals can often get us through the day in a much more elegant way.

In *The New Success* I ask readers to describe their ideal day. Setting Intentions is another step in that process. When we set an Intention for a day or an event, we are describing how we want to act and/or how we prefer it to end.

As an example, several years ago I was the training manager for a large division. Each quarter my staff gathered training requirements from the twenty training coordinators in the division and produced a report for the corporate training office, letting them know how many people in our division needed to attend specific classes. Based on these reports, the corporate office would allocate to us slots for classes in which we could enroll people. The allocations were usually around thirty percent less than the request, so the staff would do their best to spread out the seats available to the coordinators.

Naturally, this resulted in a barrage of phone calls from angry coordinators, often accusing my staff of favoritism and incompetence, neither of which was the case. I thought, "There must be a better way," and asked myself, "What is my Intention here?"

Efforts to change the corporate office were in vain, so I knew that, at least for the time being, I had to work with what I had. I really wanted the training coordinators to be satisfied that everything was being done to get them the training their people needed. I also wanted to take the pressure off my staff, since they needed to spend their time working on projects rather than calming down irate clients. My underlying Intention was to arrive at the highest solution for everyone concerned.

Keeping my Intention in mind, I remembered that when people solve their own problems, they generally like the solutions better than those imposed on them. The next time we received our allocation from corporate, I scheduled a meeting with the coordinators informing them that from now on they would, as a group, determine their allocations. I also warned them that, if they or their representatives were not at the meeting, they would receive no allocations. As I held fast to my Intention, they reluctantly agreed to attend the meeting. Many walked in grumbling.

As we progressed through the meeting, it became apparent that my approach was working. They began to trade with one another and to negotiate around each other's requirements. Within only a half-hour all the allocations were split up and agreed to. The coordinators had intelligent explanations for their bosses and there were no angry phone calls to my staff. In fact, with their new awareness, the coordinators were able to bring more power to the situation and we began receiving increased allocations from corporate.

If I had set a goal to by-God make this thing work, we would probably still be locked in mortal combat.

Where and when do we set Intentions? Anywhere there is an opportunity to interact with another person or any time we need to accomplish something.

If you hold the Intention to remember your Destiny, you will do what it takes to do so. This is actually the easy part. Holding the Intention to *live* your Destiny can be the difficult part and it will give you a good indication of how deep that Intention is. Your Intention to continue must be strong.

Intentions also help when we're in an unpleasant or difficult situation.When you're feeling frustrated, angry, or out-of-sorts, rather than fighting your way out of the problem or trying to change another person, ask yourself, "How would I prefer to feel?" Within the answer is often your solution.

Once, in a class I was teaching to a corporate client, one participant told me this story, a common one in today's workplace.

"I wake up each morning thinking of all the work we have to do. I prioritize my to-do list and work hard all day." she said, "But, at the end of the day, I am frustrated because I can't accomplish it all."

Her well-meaning classmates began giving her suggestions about how she could better utilize her time and prioritize her list further. After a couple of minutes I called, "time out" and asked, "Working hard is not a problem to you, is it?"

She said that she was a very hard worker and was backed up by her colleagues.

"Are you an organized worker?" I asked. Again the response was affirmative.

"Then, if hard work and organization are not the problems for you, why don't you influence your frustration. Tell me, rather than frustrated, how would you *prefer* to feel?"

"I would like to be satisfied with the amount I accomplish each day," she said.

"Then, instead of concentrating on how to do more work, since you're already organized, managing your time, and working hard, set an Intention at the beginning of each day to accept what you're doing as enough."

After thinking about it for a few seconds, she agreed it might be a better way to go. Although it was difficult at first, with a few days practice, she was far happier and much less frustrated.

When we approach our day from our Intention, we can free up more energy for accomplishment rather than using it for frustration, anger, and self-pity.

Our normal problem solving process looks something like this:

Problem ➔ Solution ➔ Implementation➔ Frustration

When we arrive at our solutions through Intention, however, the outcome is often much more satisfying. Try the following sequence instead:

Problem ➜ Intention ➜ Solution ➜ Implementation ➜
Less Frustration

Using Intention as an integral part of the problem-solving process not only speeds up the process by eliminating options that don't fall within the Intention parameters, but it helps to set up solutions that are more satisfying because they address your deepest needs. In addition, setting an Intention can sometimes bring you closer to the root of the problem.

## *Exercise 5:*

## *Setting Intentions for a Specific Event or Relationship*

Think about an event that is happening soon in your life. It could be a meeting or something you want to do. It could be a project you are working on or a pleasant or unpleasant anticipation. Perhaps you will be talking to someone you are uncomfortable with or to whom you are making an important presentation.

Complete the following on a three by five index card:

My Intention toward (event or person) _____is:_____

Fill out a card for each person or situation with which you are currently dealing. Intention helps us clarify what we want, where our real power in the situation rests, and what our stake in it is. Place the intention(s) you just wrote where it is easily visible when you need it.

## *Exercise 6*
### *Daily Intention*

One of the first things I do each morning when I wake up is to set an Intention for that day. Some days I need to set the Intention just to get through it in a peaceful manner. Other days I want to feel loving no matter what. Often I want to use my time effectively and in ways that further me on my path.

Your daily Intentions do not have to be lofty. In fact, the simpler the better. Remembering your Intention throughout the day will help you to step closer to your ideal life.

For instance, suppose that today I want to experience more inner peace. As I go through the day I may encounter an angry customer, an overbearing boss, whiney kids, an uncaring spouse, and soup spilled on my best suit. (Does this sound familiar to any of you?)

If I remember that my Intention is inner peace, I will consciously and subconsciously respond differently than if I didn't have this Intention. When setting and remembering Intentions becomes a habit with me, I may not get nearly as upset with all of this as I might have otherwise. This frees me to do my work more effectively while not dumping poisons into my body. It has been well documented that, when you become angry, stressed, or upset, your body manufactures chemicals that shut down and otherwise affect many of the body's processes so it can prepare for battle. During a physical battle, these hormones and other chemicals are dispersed in a manner in keeping with their functions. This is useful in hand-to-hand combat, but most of us do not engage in that very often, so the substances that were produced to help us have nowhere to go, except to stay in the body. The result can be diseases and chronic conditions that cause us much pain and suffering.

If you are internally peaceful while surrounded by upsetting situations, you can probably resolve the difficulties much more easily than if you were to become upset. You will also provide a model for how to behave in a productive manner. Have you ever noticed how people don't remain in negative behavior very long if you are coming from an inner power of peace?

This is just one example of an Intention you may wish to set. I have found this to be particularly powerful when combined with the Ideal Day Exercise described in my book, *The New Success.* One of my clients, after trying this process, found that, as she got to the end of a particularly trying day, she was not drained either physically or emotionally because she had preset her responses by setting an Intention and describing an Ideal Day. Here is how you can do it too:

## *Exercise 7:*
### *Ideal Day*

Record the following in your Destiny notebook:

*Step 1:* Complete the sentence:
My Intention just for today is: _____
_____

*Step 2:* Write a description of how you would like your day to go. Pretend you are writing an overview of a movie script in which you are describing the day to a movie producer.

*Step 3:* Read the Intention and description out loud. If this is not possible, read them as mindfully as you can, getting into the feel of it as much as possible.

## *Exercise 8:*
### *Life Intentions*

We all live life by certain principles formed through our education, experiences and beliefs. By understanding what they are, we can use them to set Intentions for how we will live our entire lives. By paying attention to what our most important principles are, and doing what we can to live by these and our Intentions, many of our decisions about what to do are made easier. And, as we are reminded by a clearly spoken Intention what is most important, we find our behavior and our responses becoming more and more consistent.

In your Destiny notebook:

**Step 1:** Write five principles by which you live your life.

**Step 2:** Write a life Intention that encompasses these principles.

**Step 3:** Write three ways you demonstrate this Intention.

Keep a journal in your Destiny Notebook to help you track your Intentions and your responses. In addition, keep notes on how your life is changing as a result.

ॐ    ॐ    ॐ

My client, Tory, had been frustrated because she was not generating enough money from her business as a piano teacher. We reviewed her schedule and added up the number of students she was teaching. She had more than enough students. In fact, she was working more than was necessary to be a success. The problem stemmed from her charging so little per lesson, and giving away so many lessons, that she was unable to care for herself and her children.

I first suggested that she raise her rates in accordance with the current "market." She argued that many of her students would leave her.

I then persuaded her to give free lessons only to one or two to people who loved them but were destitute. This would be her tithe. I then recommended that she notify those who really didn't appreciate her lessons that they would have to pay for them.

Our next step was for her to articulate her Intentions for how she wanted to live her life. She said the most important thing was a decent income and time to spend with her children so they would have a proper upbringing.

She realized that letting go of those students who didn't pay and didn't appreciate her would open some time for her family, but she refused to raise her rates, saying it was too big of a risk. The more she worked on her Intention, however, the more resolute she became about giving her family a better life.

Finally, she agreed to charge *new* students the higher rates and to tell the current students that in six months her rates would be increased.

The strangest things happened once she clearly understood her Intention and began to live by it. Several of her students who had not been paying volunteered to pay for the lessons. When students left, their slots were immediately filled with new ones paying the higher rates. And, most of her current students felt the rate increase was justified.

None of this happened until she set an Intention about how she would live her life.

On another occasion, a certain gentleman wanted to attend a retreat I was co-leading. He didn't feel he could afford the full tuition, yet after he heard me speak about creating, he consequently decided to register for the retreat by putting down a deposit. In doing so, he set an Intention.

As he was about to make the check out for the deposit, he heard a voice inside his head saying, "Pay the full amount NOW!" The more he tried to ignore it, the louder the voice seemed to get. Finally, he gave up and wrote the check for the full amount.

Within three days, a former client, who owed him money and from whom he had despaired of ever receiving payment, sent him a check for the full amount of the debt. It not only covered the cost of the retreat, there was money left over for a tithe and for other items.

Coincidence? Maybe. Probably not.

*Chapter 4*

*Vision*

When I use the word "Vision" to describe methods of remembering and manifesting destiny, I am talking not just about using our physical eyes to see. I am also referring to the use of all our outer and inner senses to create a whole picture.

Learning to use Vision is important because it helps us to tune with more clarity into the "frequency" of our spiritual radios.

Remembering your destiny is not just about sitting around on your velvet pillow waiting for a vision to happen. It is more like a dance. You are given a realization or vision, and you must do what you can to follow it and create it. Then you are given more. Sometimes you are given just a glimpse of your destiny, so you must be alert. Developing the ability to see is simply another vital tool to use in manifesting this wonderful destiny for which you were created.

Some people have said to me, "I have never been able to see with my mind's eye. I hear and feel, but don't see."

Developing Vision can be a real challenge if it is not one of your dominant means of gathering information. We all learn by seeing, hearing and doing. Most of us use one more often than the other two, although if we develop the ability to learn by using all three, we will have a more complete experience.

Some books and teachers use the old exercise of looking at a picture and recreating it, bit by bit, in your mind with your eyes closed as a way of developing vision. This is a fine exercise and I recommend it if you have not developed this faculty, but I will not dwell on this exercise, since you can find it in so many places.

Rather, we're going to work with other techniques to help you develop a more finely tuned sense of Vision. Even if you, like me, see a movie every time you close your eyes, it is still a good idea to perform exercises to keep the skill sharpened. It's like being born with a talent for music. If you never practice, you can still get by on a rudimentary level. But, to become accomplished and stay that way, you must consistently work at it.

The following exercise will help you to obtain a vision of your destiny. (It is also helpful when working with World Service.)

## *Meditation 3:*
### *The Movie*

Become still, relax, and close your eyes. Imagine that you are going to attend the premier of a new hit movie. See yourself getting ready, wearing whatever makes you feel elegant. This will be a big night!

It is time to leave now. As you walk out your front door, a limousine pulls up to get you. This is unlike any limousine you have ever seen. It is made of light and shimmers softly as twilight descends.

Your driver floats around the car and opens the door for you. You feel absolutely safe as you climb in and seat yourself in the plush interior. From behind the wheel, the driver asks if you are ready. When you are ready, say, "Let's go."

Rather than moving forward, the limo gently begins to rise. As you look out you see your street and dwelling disappear below. You see our solar system fly by as you approach the outer universe. As you watch the stars move past the windows, you find yourself becoming more and more relaxed and looking forward to the movie.

At last the journey is over. The driver opens your door. As you emerge from the car, you see yourself in front of a huge movie palace. It shines and glows, its radiant interior beckons to you. A being escorts you inside and you move into the lobby.

You notice that you are the only one attending the premier. Your escort informs you that the movie has been produced for you alone. It is called, "Your Destiny."

You walk, unescorted, into the theater. You look around at the opulent surroundings. At one end of the room is a giant screen. Scattered throughout are lush, comfortable sofas and chairs. The carpeting is thick and plush, the lighting and colors soft and relaxing.

You select a place to sit and prepare for viewing the movie. The lights dim and the screen lights up. On the screen is the title with your name at the top. "Your Destiny" fills the bottom half of the screen. The title fades and the movie begins.

Watch the movie now as your destiny begins to unfold on the screen. Stay for as long as you like.

When the movie has finished for you, rise and walk back to the car. The trip back home takes only a few moments. When you arrive, take a deep breath, open your eyes and awake, refreshed from your experience.

1.  For the next several minutes write every-thing you can remember from the above exercise. In your notebook write what you saw, felt, heard, or intuited. Don't worry if any of it made sense. Just write it all down.
2.  Do this exercise for several days, each day writing all you can remember about your experience.
3.  When you feel a sense of completion with the Visualization exercise, read and re-read your notes, seeing if you can discern a pattern. Highlight or circle those items which seem significant to you.

4. On a separate sheet of paper, copy the Destiny Statement you developed in Chapter Two. On that same sheet of paper, copy the items you have just highlighted. Using all the information on this sheet, rewrite your Destiny Statement and any insights you may have gained about it.

You are now gaining depth with your Destiny Statement and getting a better idea about your destiny. As I have said earlier, you will often get only glimpses of your Destiny. Other times you may see an entire panorama. Understanding Visioning and learning to recognize these glimpses moves you along more quickly.

❧ ❧ ❧

The following exercise will help you build your Visioning skill. It is an ancient exercise but since most people I encounter are not familiar with it, I'm including it here.

## *Exercise 9:*
### *The Color in the Flame*

Light a candle. Focus on the flame for a few moments. Then, see if you can turn the flame green as you look at it. Some of you are saying, "What do you mean, turn the flame green? A candle flame is yellow. What a dumb exercise!" You're right. The candle flame will not actually turn green, but, in concentrating on it, you can actually trick your brain into seeing it as green.

Again, this is to help you build a skill. When you have successfully seen the candle flame as green, try other colors, such as red, purple, or blue. Many students report that some colors seem easier than others, so if you are not successful with one, try the others. Keep practicing this exercise daily until it becomes easy for you.

If you are a person who does not Visualize naturally, this exercise will prove especially valuable to you in helping you develop this skill. If your dominant style is hearing, feeling, or moving, Visualization will no doubt never become your primary tool. However, developing the faculty will enhance all your experiences. The same goes for those who are primarily visual. Developing your kinesthetic, auditory and intuitive sides will intensify your ability to learn and create.

⚝ ⚝ ⚝

Once in meditation, I was shown a very powerful exercise combining Articulation and Visualization. I still use it and the people who have practiced it to its full extent have experienced nothing short of miracles in their lives. Let me caution you: don't do this unless you really want changes in your life!

## *Exercise 10:*
## *Six Month Vision Statement*

You will need a candle and some paper upon which to write.

When you first begin this exercise, sit for a few moments and think about how you would like the coming year to go. Don't limit yourself. Just give yourself permission to daydream a little.

When you feel a sense of completion with that, write out a concept for each of the next six months, describing the *results* you want to see for each month. Don't worry about *activities* yet. Write approximately two paragraphs for the coming month and one for each of the next five.

Six months is a comfortable time period for me and seems to work well for my students. It is enough time for the universe to rearrange itself to accommodate you, but not so long that you feel trapped. You may have a solid idea of where you want to be in a year or even five years. If so, write that at the top of the page as your overriding thought. (However, be prepared to modify it!)

You may find that a year at a time works better for you. Perhaps, if you're going through a difficult time or unsure about exactly what you want, you may wish to work on a week at a time, maybe even a day at a time. (Believe me, many times in my life, a day was all I could handle!)

When I'm doing this, I don't get too hung up on "reality." (According to my husband, I've never been particularly concerned with this to begin with.) In other words, some of the things I write seem outrageous or impossible. Never fear.

When you are satisfied with your Vision Statement (about two typewritten pages for a six-month period), read it out loud until you are comfortable with even the most exorbitant parts of it, revising it until it just "feels" right. (It may be best to seek privacy while you do this.) Then place the statement in the front of your Destiny Journal so it is the first thing you see when you open the book.

For each of the next fifteen days do the following at least once a day:

1. Open your book to your six-month vision.
2. Light the candle. This may sound a little woo-woo, but, actually, lighting the candle puts your subconscious on notice that something is about to happen. I have been doing this for more than twenty-five years, so, when I light that candle, my subconscious really knows it must pay attention. You may feel more comfortable ringing a small bell or putting on soothing music. From now on, be consistent with your signal to your subconscious. It really works!
3. Read the entire vision out loud each day. Then concentrate on the month just ahead, watching it unfold in your mind, experiencing the emotions and the joy of it. Become excited about the people you will help and the happiness and abundance you

will create. At some point you will feel that this part of the process is complete. At that point let your intense Visioning work rest for a few days.

4. The final step in this process is the most important: Let go of the outcome. I have found that, as I bathe my subconscious mind in the overall picture of what I want, it begins to work on arranging the outcome that works best for me. In almost every case, the different outcome is better. Plus, I don't feel nearly the stress, nor the sense of failure I once did if things don't work out exactly as I had pictured.

5. When the current month ends, add a month, keeping a sort of "rolling" six-month vision going.

The Intention with which you approach this exercise determines, to a great degree, the results you attain. Among my clients, the ones who are willing to follow this procedure are the ones who accomplish the most.

The first time I was shown this, I was at a point where I really didn't know if I could continue doing what I was doing. I had had so many setbacks in my business that I was questioning whether I had really gauged my World Service correctly. Within a week of starting the Six-Month Vision Statement exercise, I had so much business that I actually had to revise my statement so I could get some sleep. I asked God to please bring me clients for the following months and shut of the spigot for the current one. I found that several of the items I had listed came to me much sooner than I had expected. I lost interest in others, realizing that they were a reflection of my fears or sense of lack.

When I first started this exercise, I had to revise my six-month statement completely about every two months. However, every time I revised it, I found my clarity increasing and my knowledge about what I wanted growing. If you aren't sure what to write because you don't know what you want in the next six months, my advice is to practice this exercise anyway, doing the best you can. You will find it will aid you greatly as you proceed. If you persist, your Vision Statements evolves with more and more clarity.

Include relationships, spiritual growth, and personal life in your Vision as well as World Service. Keeping a balance is an important part of this process.

For many people this sort of activity does not come naturally. Some work for several months before they begin to see results. But, if they are persistent, the payoff is astonishing. Most people see some sort of difference very quickly if they are sincere and consistent. If you are having difficulty with this, you will be able to add more skills when you get to the chapter on Projection.

Working with this process, I find that my goals are becoming more and more in alignment with who I really am and what, at my deepest level, I want to do in life. My daily "to-do" lists are much more Focused and I seem to concentrate more easily on the activities that will contribute to positive outcomes. Try it for six months. Your life will change!

༅ ༅ ༅

I received a lovely letter from a woman who committed to the six-month Visioning process. She gave me permission to share it with you.

*Using the technique of writing down what I want to have or to happen in monthly increments for six months has been easy and difficult at the same time. It's difficult because of having to put on paper the desires of my heart. This is probably the most important function of this method; committing to what I want.*

*The daily review and updating (or course correction) kept me Focused and clear so that when my heart's desires appeared, I instantly recognized them.*

*I realize that it is incredibly important to say, 'Thank you' to each desire that manifests, no matter how large or small. I must even say 'thank you' to those desires that appear which I did not even know I wanted on a conscious level. It must be that once I am into the creating mode, God works on all levels, even those of which I am not aware.*

When I contacted her, I asked her if things had gone smoothly while she practiced the Visioning process. She responded that it had been a very bumpy road. I told her that, if things appear to be falling completely apart when doing this process, it is because everything is readjusting in order to create what is desired. Sometimes it feels much more like destruction than construction. Sometimes, however, an unstable or decrepit structure must be torn down to make way for the beautiful new edifice that takes its place.

*Chapter 5*

# *Projection*

Projection is using the energy available to us to form that which is desired. Jesus was, of course, an expert at this. For years I used the term, "creation" to describe the process covered in this chapter. However, because energy can be neither created nor destroyed, I now use the term "Projection" as it more closely describes the process. Many times I use the words interchangeably. As we Project our Vision into the field of energy, it then begins to form into that which we want.

Projection, as used in the Destiny Process, helps us to bring into manifestation that which we have Articulated and Visioned.

One of the most compelling examples of Projection comes from a little man in India named Sai Baba. He routinely creates a sort of dust, seemingly out of nothing, that flows freely from his hands. All scientific efforts to discern the origin of his creation have failed. Yet, hundreds of stories emerge from his ashram from reliable witnesses who have seen him produce everything from camera film to precious jewelry. In other words, he has mastered the art of Projection.

Modern science has demonstrated that atoms react to thoughts. In one experiment, observers were able to actually track an atom that moved in response to another researcher's thoughts. Although this phenomena was discovered accidentally, it certainly rearranged the thinking of those present.

Learning to work with energy is important to your Destiny Process, as it can accelerate results you wish to attain. Once you have remembered some or all of your destiny, it is important to begin right away to work with this knowledge and to outpicture as much as you can. It is eminently practical, as you need spend less energy manifesting, freeing up more energy to fulfill your destiny.

We can work with this available energy in our own creation exercises. Cameras have been developed which photograph the energy around our bodies. In fact, we are walking energy fields, just waiting to produce.

Many people, myself included, have actually seen this energy. It usually takes a little practice, but it can be done. (Several people I know can "see" it with their eyes closed, even though they can't perceive it by looking at another person with their physical eyes.)

I discovered one easy way for me to see my own energy quite by accident. I had just returned from a vigorous run and was in my garden talking to my plants. When I put my hands on either side of a plant I was about to bless, I noticed what looked like little sparks dancing in the air between my hands. I watched, fascinated for about ten minutes, when it faded. For the next several weeks, after each run, I would space my hands about a foot apart, facing each other, and watch the dance of energy sparks. I occasionally perform this exercise, just because it's fun.

I don't know why I was able to see the energy so well after running. Perhaps it was because I had so much oxygen coursing through me and so much vital energy released through running. I would be interested in hearing from anyone with similar experiences.

Before this incident, however, I spent some years practicing the art of seeing energy around people, plants, even inanimate objects. I must admit that it was never a huge priority, so my practice was somewhat spotty. It was less important to me to become an expert at seeing energy than at using it.

By now I can, at any time, sense and see this energy between my hands, even if I haven't been running. (It's just more sparkly after vigorous exercise.) I have further discovered that it *is* important to the creation process that we become aware of the energy, because then it makes it easier to work with.

The first step in becoming an expert in Projection is to become accustomed to the energy itself. For starters, try the following exercise every day for two weeks. By the end of that time, you will have a much better idea of what this energy is like than if I were to spend weeks trying to describe it to you.

## *Exercise 11:*
### *Seeing the Energy*

Seat yourself in a darkened, candle-lit room. Sit in a comfortable way for a minute or two until you feel relaxed. Rub your hands together vigorously until they become heated. Slowly separate them, palms facing inward, until they are no more than six inches apart. After a little practice, you should be able to feel that the air between your hands feels somewhat denser than normal. Gently push your hands closer until you can feel the boundaries of the energy.

After you practice for a while you can get your hands further and further apart with the energy field feeling stronger and stronger. While you're experimenting, you may also begin to see faint threads or clouds of light, barely discernible between your hands. If I have not been working much with energy and need to get the "feel" back, I do this exercise and it gets me right back in the groove.

You may do this exercise in a fully lighted room, but it may be a little more difficult to see the energy. As you look through the space between your hands, you may see something resembling heat waves coming off the pavement on a hot day.

Also, look at this field after a vigorous 45 minutes of exercise and you may also see the energy lights dancing between your hands.

ଫ    ଫ    ଫ

Thoughts have energy. We have more than two decades of scientific research showing us that plants and animals respond on a physiological level to our thoughts.

Research has also proven that people who are prayed for respond positively, *even when they do not know it is happening.* Cameras can actually take pictures of the energy fields surrounding our bodies as well as those of plants and animals.

However, despite this evidence, most people don't know how to work with this energy. It all sounds so mumbo-jumbo and like "occult magic" we've all been warned about.

When studying the Aramaic (the language of Jesus) scriptures, we find that Jesus not only knew how to use this energy, but he used energy to perform his healing. He knew how to harness this power and he told us we could not only accomplish similar feats, but, in fact, do more.

I use Jesus as an example so that you understand that it is not an occult-type practice. In fact, it has been used by the best.

Therapeutic Touch is being applied by an increasing number of nurses and is proving to be an effective healing aid. The practice of Reiki, a form of energetic healing is gaining acceptance and respect. (In my case, a Reiki healer "drew" a 102 degree fever out of my body in about thirty seconds, just by putting her hands on my back. It made a believer out of me!)

This Reiki healer knows how to Focus the energy from the universe through her hands and into the areas of the body that need healing. The problem is, since we can't see energy, we often resist working with it on a conscious level. What you may not realize, however, is that you are working with energy every moment of the day. We manipulate this energy with every thought we think, every word we utter, and every movement we make.

If you've ever seen a photograph of a person's energy field, you will notice that the size and colors vary according to the health and mood of the person. Each individual has his or her own "signature" field as well. Some people can see these colors and patterns without the camera's help. Most of these people have practiced in order to use this skill and you can also develop this ability, at least to a limited degree.

The following exercise will help you to see or sense the colors of the energy fields that make up your body. Developing this skill is useful in several ways. First, when you learn to "see" colors in your energy field or that of others, you may be able to identify areas that may need attention, often before symptoms appear.

As you become more proficient in this practice, you will often be able to "read" the moods of others so you can work with them better. One person I know is very good at reading the energy fields of clients and can tell if they are being honest with her or not, just by the changes and colors of their energy fields. She has learned to identify the colors that are linked to truth and those  connected with deception. A useful skill indeed!

The better you are at becoming aware of energy fields and energy patterns, the greater your skill at manipulating and projecting that which you prefer to happen in your life.

## *Exercise 12:*
## *Energy Fields*

Make a copy of the outline of the person on Page 80 You may wish to make several copies so you can perform this exercise a number of times to gain proficiency. Get out some crayons or colored pencils in as many different colors as possible.

Become silent and close your eyes. Starting at the top of your head, imagine that you are going to see the colors in your own energy field. In your mind, slowly scan your body from head to toe getting a feeling for the colors, the sizes of their fields and their locations. You may see the colors or you may just sense them.

When you have finished your Visualization, use the crayons to fill in the colors as you saw or sensed them, on the drawing.

You may find that you sensed only one or two areas or none at all. Or, you may find your drawing leaping from the page in living color. Any result (or non-result) is fine. You may find that you sensed energy patterns rather than colors. If that is so, draw those.

It is difficult to explain to you exactly what your drawing should look like. There is really no wrong way to do this. When I do this exercise with groups in classes or retreats, the expressions are as varied as the people themselves. Yet, all were appropriate.

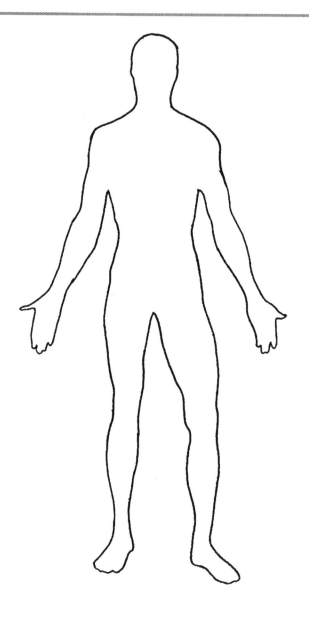

***Alternate One:*** You may find that you had no experience at all. Or you may just wish to try this as another way
to tune into your own energy. In this exercise, simply
become quiet and still your mind. Without closing your
eyes, simply begin to color the picture as you feel led to do.
You may be surprised at how you are guided to one color or
another. This will also help you to strengthen your ability to
tune in and is an alternate Access exercise.

***Alternate Two:*** Tune into people and try to imagine
their energy fields. If you are in the privacy of your home,
you may wish to color their fields. This is also a great
exercise if you are sitting in a boring meeting or lecture.

***Alternate Three:*** Get together with a friend. Ask that
person to read this section. Then, tune into each other's
energy fields, using the colors as in the previous exercises.

***Alternate Four:*** Before you go into a meeting, think
about the person with whom you will be dealing the most.
As you sense this person's energy fields, ask how you may
best serve and interact with that individual. Do not use this
technique to manipulate the other person for your own gain,
as it will eventually backfire. All that you do must be for the
highest good of all concerned.

***Alternate Five:*** The next time someone close to you is
feeling ill, ask if you may lay your hands on her and pray
for her (or, if she is enlightened at all, tell her you want to
practice healing with energy). If you word it right, you
won't make the person too nervous. This is, of course, an
ancient practice, applied in all societies and religions to
some extent.

The easiest method is to put your hand on top of the person's head or on the shoulders. Some people like to rub their hands together to get energy flowing.

*Step One:* Close your eyes and sense what you can about the person's energy patterns. You may get a sense of some energy being "trapped" somewhere in the body or an impression. Depending on the person's reception to the process, you may share what you sense.

*Step Two:* Feel energy coming in through the top of your head, moving through you and out your hands into the person's body. Don't worry about placing your hands on the exact spot of injury or illness. The energy will go where it is needed. Keep in mind that God, not you, is the source of the energy. Ask that this energy flow to where it will do the most good and stay detached from the outcome. Any time you perform this exercise, healing will occur. However, you may not always be able to see it physically. Just know that what you are doing is for the highest good of all concerned.

When you first begin, you may feel nothing, but as you practice, you will sense, not only the source of the illness or energy, but you will know when your "treatment" is finished. You will feel a subtle energy shift.

Some individuals with a talent for this particular sort of healing find great currents of energy running through them. Others can immediately "see" or feel the source of the disease. Still others receive messages about healing applications.

It doesn't matter if you experience any of the above. Any time you work with someone using this technique and you sincerely wish that individual to benefit from it, there will be good done on some level. You are also benefitting, as you become healthier each time you use energy in this manner.

ॐ   ॐ   ॐ

Have you ever "sensed" something about another person, such as she was ill or was hiding something? Some women have an uncanny knack for sensing when another woman is pregnant, even though there's no physical evidence. Masters of the Oriental art of Qi Gong can diagnose illness simply by looking at the patient. They are all tuning into the energy fields of the individuals, just like you are.

You can also use this energy to harm yourself. I have noticed an alarming trend in today's world toward what I call "Victiming." This is the art of making oneself a victim of circumstances, events, or illness, rather than marshalling this energy to be a healing force.

"Victiming" is an easy practice to fall into and I know of no one who does not occasionally, even subtly, stumble into its trap. When we behave as if we were a victim, we close off many of the avenues open to us. Any time we feel ourselves to be anything but triumphant we are engaging in "Victiming" and, like Peter, denying the Christ.

ॐ   ॐ   ॐ

Once I was conducting a panel discussion on my tele-vision show regarding a certain health condition. The condition is painful to be sure. As I listened to each indi-vidual, it became very clear to me that the one who seemed to be handling it the best was the one who had chosen to take control of her destiny. Yes, she was experiencing pain, but, instead of dwelling on it, she took action to get through it and manage it. The others, who were not as pro-active, consistently referred to themselves as "victims" of the condition.

I am not making light of things that happen to people that are genuinely tragic. I'm talking about those times when we create the condition for ourselves or overplay what life does to us.

Victiming is usually characterized by a "poor me" or an "it's not my fault" or and "I just can't help it" attitude. It can be insidious, creeping up on us without warning, silently, like the thief in the night. We often don't recognize when we're engaged in it.

Have you ever gotten yourself into an obligation, then regretted it? But, rather than fulfilling it and moving on, felt sorry for yourself while in the middle of it?

One dear man I know had the habit of agreeing to work on projects with people who were not in his best interest, even knowing in advance he would regret it. Sometime during the project, he would get fed up and, rather than simply finishing it in his own power, would get more and more frustrated until he would blow up, often damaging the relationship beyond repair. He would then spend hours (days, weeks, months, years) reliving the experience, telling others what a horrible person the other one was. After a while, those who knew him would just smile indulgently, thinking, "Well, here he goes again."

Fortunately, he began to see these patterns and turned down proposals from people who did not contribute to his highest good. Now he is working on more and more projects with people who are a good fit for him, and his life is much happier (as are the lives of those around him).

Another person I knew had the habit of getting herself into situations and projects that overwhelmed her. Rather than gracefully exit or delegate part of the load, she would either injure herself or become ill, rendering herself incapable of continuing and leaving others to pick up the pieces. After realizing her pattern, she became more selective about her choices and was able to go on with her life with her health and body intact.

Although these are somewhat extreme cases, we can all look at areas in our lives where we play the victim.

For instance, have you ever caught yourself saying any of the following, even in passing:

"I can't."

"I don't know why I even try."

"My life just isn't worth much."

"I'm such a klutz."

"I'm really not very talented."

"I eat when I'm under stress."

"I don't have time for _____"

"He/she/it prevented me from getting what I wanted."

"I can't do anything about it."

"He _____," "She _____," They _____,"

All these are examples of "Victiming." And they can become habits. One woman I know consistently says, "I can't" before trying anything. Although I suppose it gets her off the hook, it certainly limits her life and turns off people from even asking her to participate in the very activities she would enjoy.

Sometimes "Victiming" can look like someone else is at fault. For instance, is there anyone who is keeping you from realizing your goals? Is there a boss, spouse, parent, child or friend who seems to stand in your way? If you say, "Yes," you are engaging in "Victiming." You see, when you are on the road to your true destiny, it is so powerful that no one can truly block your path. Except you.

Others may *seem* to be in the way, but they are just reflections of your own fears. If you can't get around them, or work with them, it may be time to try a new direction. But the first place to look is inside and deal with your fears first.

It is very easy to slip into "Victiming" when we're tired or not feeling well. At that point, we may slip into, "Oh, what's the use" or other victim phrases. Fatigue is the enemy of courage, but if you are aware of the syndrome, you can stop it before it begins.

My husband and I are pretty good at reminding each other of "victimizing." We both work at getting through it as quickly as possible. When one isn't feeling well, the other gets a sympathetic look on his or her face and says in a pitiful voice, "Poor thee, poor thee." The other nods with a sad look. This gentle teasing helps us remember that, even though we don't feel well, we'll be okay. And, it's a loving way of letting the other person know we really do care about how he or she feels.

But, in some cases, the drama of being a victim pays off handsomely. It can often bring us attention. We took our young granddaughter to a restaurant with a children's play area. It was warm and she had overdone it to the point where she became ill for a while. (Isn't that what grandparents are for?) Once we got home, she was fine and was content coloring. My husband came into the room and asked her how she was feeling. Immediately her demeanor changed. With a heavy sigh and a "dying swan" expression on her face, she looked through big eyes and said, "Oh, not so well." He patted her on the head and said, "Well, when you feel better, we'll go to the park." She experienced an immediate miracle of healing.

In her case, the drama didn't pay off, so she changed the script. But, can you think of times when "Victiming" has paid off for you and others? We all can. Unfortunately, for many people it becomes a habit to the point of interfering with a life fully realized. And, we may all have pockets of life where we are, even unknowingly, playing victim.

This is why it's so important to develop the habit of stopping this kind of thinking in the beginning stages. Once again, our old friend, Awareness, steps in. Here's an exercise to help you become more aware of this habit.

## Exercise 13:
### Victiming

Look back at the previous forty-eight hours. Think about times when you may have, even fleetingly, slipped into victim-thinking or talking. In your notebook write down as many as you can remember.

During the week, keep a log in your personal planner or your Destiny Notebook of each time you slip into "Victiming." If you are unsure if it's "Victiming," write it down anyway and analyze it later.

After you've done this long enough to sense a pattern, review your notes. Ask yourself the following questions:

- Is there a pattern to my "Victiming?" Do I engage in it when I'm lonely, overwhelmed, blocked, frustrated or stressed?
- How does it manifest? Do I complain, whine, sleep, eat, drink, withdraw, or lash out?
- Why do I think I have adopted this pattern?
- What can I do to become more aware of it while it's happening?
- What healthy steps could I take to diffuse it?

When you first become aware of your habit, allow yourself some time simply to be able to recognize it without judgement. As you go through the questions above, you may become more enlightened about it. Strangely, being aware of it can often be all that's needed to stop the behavior and allow you to move to a more healthy level of living.

ক ক ক

Many have used the following exercise to bring successfully that which they wish into their lives. It's fun and helps you to get the feeling of Projecting your desires into the universe. Before you begin, decide exactly what you want to manifest. Work with only one idea at a time. When you attempt to work with more than one idea, the energy becomes diffused, producing vague or even undesirable results. When I first began projecting my desires consciously, I said, "I'm such a mess! I need everything!" Ignoring the advice of working with one thing at a time, I pictured all my good happening at once. The results were a little like that of the sorcerer's apprentice. I got results, but not exactly as I had pictured. When I settled down and focused on one or two critical items I was most in need of, everything else fell into place naturally. If you wish to project more than that, perform the exercise for each one separately. I would suggest a total of no more than three, even after you become proficient at the practice.

Remember the following when working with Projection:

1.  You must never attempt to make another person do anything. Don't ask for John to fall in love with you or Susie to pay you the money she owes. If you are seeking a mate to fulfill your desires, visualize the perfect mate coming to you. If you ask for John, you may very well get him, then find out he's not such a great catch after all. If someone owes you money, let go of the money coming from that person. Ask that all financial matters be settled quickly and in divine order. That can free you from the

negative energy generated about the person who owes you money and frees other avenues to open up so you experience no loss.

2. You must never ask for something that will harm another. That which you project will come back to you, so never send out anything you don't want.

3. As much as possible, perform the projection exercises without fear as to the outcome. If you send your thoughts out with fear and chaos, that is what will return. If you are able to calm yourself enough to be peaceful, even for a few minutes, your results will reflect that.

Before I realized how powerful our thoughts and energy projections are, I would not have paid much attention to the power of ideas. After years of experience with this practice, however, I know how important it is not to project fear or negativity. Please pay attention to the caveats expressed above .

## *Exercise 14:*
### *Energy Ball*

Become quiet. Form a picture or symbol of what you want in your mind. If you have a photograph of the object or symbol, place it in front of you where you can look at it to get an even clearer picture of it. Rub your hands together until they become warm. With palms facing each other, slowly move your hands until they are about twelve inches apart. Gently push in until you feel the boundary of the energy field. Play with this energy until it feels like you are holding an "energy ball."

As you hold this ball, in your mind's eye project the picture or symbol of your desire in the middle of it, surrounded by energy. It will seem as if you are holding your desire between your hands. When you feel complete, toss the ball up to the universe as if you were making a free throw in basketball. As you do this, picture the universe sending the three-dimensional version of your desire back to you in wonderful ways. Give thanks and let the ball float off on its own accord. Know that your request is being handled in ways that you needn't worry about.

Repeat this exercise once or twice a day until you feel complete with it. Act on guidance you receive about it. As with any of the exercises, release concern about the outcome.

୫   ୫   ୫

When you become a part of the creative energy, things happen. When you use it to fulfill your destiny, things happen as if by magic.

*Chapter 6*

*Allowance*

Several years ago, I was given a glimpse of my destiny in its full flower. It terrified me. I saw myself writing books and leading seminars, helping people to discover their greatness. It was too grandiose, too far beyond my reach, too much for me to handle. At least I thought so.

I finally realized that it would happen only if I allowed it. At that point I began my submission to the will of God. I'm still working at it, falling off here, stubbing my toe there, but always getting up again and saying, "Nevertheless, Thy will be done."

Neither your destiny nor mine can manifest if we try to make it happen. We're kind of like a visitor I had a few years ago.

I had returned home from an appointment and was listening to the last of my phone messages, when I heard a curious scraping noise coming from inside the house. Concerned, and a little nervous, I began quietly to seek its source. The scraping and scratching continued as I tiptoed into the family room. At first I thought it was coming from the furnace ducts, but I then realized it was originating from within the glass-enclosed fireplace. I slowly approached it and peeked inside. Behind the glass screen, peering from behind the mesh curtain was a squirrel with the biggest eyes I've ever seen. He (and I) had no idea how he got there, and it was pretty obvious he didn't want to remain in confinement.

I spoke to him in low and what I hoped were reassuring tones as I opened the slider leading outside. I then slowly opened the glass fireplace door and the wire mesh, still speaking and moving slowly and softly.

He streaked out, thinking he was free. It immediately became apparent, that he now faced a new, and perhaps more complex, problem. Surveying his new environs, he scampered to the sofa, explored it thoroughly, ran into the dining room, up one of the chairs, across the buffet and down again, and on into the living room.

He made a bee line for the windows, only to face bitter disappointment when he found they were closed. He saw me following him and bounded across a table, leaving a wounded fern in his wake. Streaking again across the sofa and coffee table, he completed another lap of the living room and raced back to the family room.

I gently herded him to the kitchen where he happily greeted the door that had been open the entire time. As he hit the vinyl kitchen floor, his feet were running at about 3,000 rpm's but his forward progress was almost nil. He finally slowed down and escaped to freedom and the sunflower seeds awaiting him on the patio.

I sometimes feel like that squirrel, racing frantically from one thing to another, spinning my wheels on life's linoleum and going nowhere. But, when I finally stop to listen, I easily hear a voice saying, "The door is over here. You just have to walk through it."

Not too long ago I threw a big fiftieth anniversary party for my parents. I had planned it for some time. However, two months before the party, our beautiful club house burned down, so we were compelled to have it at our house (a *lot* more work!). One month before the party, my father suffered a heart attack. The next day, my beautiful grandchild was born. Oh yeah, I also got attacked by a dog somewhere in there. It was beginning to look like a recipe for certain disaster. However, knowing the power of words, I just kept saying, "I can Allow this to be easy." After eliminating what was unnecessary for the party, I simply Allowed it to happen. Two or three friends stepped forward to help. My son and his wife brought their family (including the new baby) over and also pitched in. My mother-in-law flew in and helped. Although we certainly did the work, it all seemed to flow easily. And, yes, my father recovered beautifully and had a wonderful time. Because of the heart attack we were all even more thankful and in a celebration mood. I could have created great drama (of which I am more than capable), but decided to let it be fun and easy instead. And we got rave reviews from all the guests!

When we practice Allowance, we consciously put ourselves in the natural flow of life. We realize that fighting the natural order of life drains our energy and leaves us without the strength to continue in a healthy manner.

Allowance does not mean that we simply sit on a velvet pillow meditating until Spirit drops a wonderful life in our laps. It means that we live life rather than fight it.

I had just returned from a session on marketing for professional speakers. As I discussed some of the suggestions with a colleague, I mentioned that it seemed like there was a lot of struggle involved with what one person was talking about. My colleague nodded in agreement and said, "About five years ago we quit aggressive marketing. We just turned everything over to God. Although we still send out flyers and develop great materials for people, once we decided to allow the good to come in, it has done so."

I know for a fact that my colleague and her husband did not just sit back and wait for God to do all the work. They did everything that was to be done by them — developed excellent programs, gave excellent customer service, and charged a fair price for their services. But they gave up struggle. And that left a whole lot of room for the good stuff.

Several years ago I was interviewing a man on my TV show. He introduced the concept to me of completely giving up struggle. He said that, at first, giving up struggle was a real struggle because it had been such an important part of his life. But, when he realized how much energy and time he devoted to it, he determined that he was going to sail through his days without the struggle. That freed so up much time, he was able to devote himself to the projects that were dear to his heart.

Although I had been familiar with the concept of letting go of struggle, I had not made much of a conscious effort to do so and was happily ensconced in my dramas, struggling contentedly away. During the week that followed the taping I made an effort (struggling again!) to notice how often I slid into struggling. What a revelation! I realized that I was struggling with almost everything that came my way. I decided that each day, when I caught myself struggling, I would stop what I was doing, take a deep breath and say to myself, "I can move through this with ease."

My life changed immediately. At once, I began to have more fun. For a while I would often struggle for several hours before I realized what I was doing. Then, when I would just Allow events to unfold, peacefully doing my part, things went more smoothly.

Then something happened that really changed my perspective. I was working on two projects simultaneously, both due three days apart. Nothing was going right with the one that seemed the most urgent. [As I noticed myself becoming more and more frustrated with things out of my control, I stopped.] I took a deep breath and listened for an answer, holding an Intention to follow the guidance I received. I felt directed to move on to the other project. At first I was afraid to do so, as I did not want the first project to be late. Sticking with my Intention, however, I followed the guidance and moved on. The second project flowed beautifully. Just as I was finishing it, I received two phone calls. The first was from the director of the number one project. He told me he had to leave town for four days unexpectedly, so would I mind waiting until his return to bring him the report. The second was from the manager of the project I had been guided to finish. She asked if I could complete the work a day early as the meeting to review it had been moved up. Since I was almost finished, it was no problem. Everything fell into place.

Now, when something just won't go right, I stop and ask myself, "What needs to change?" Recently, I took a job to a copy service to get a large order filled rather quickly. I was told that it would take several hours. Because I was running errands while they were supposed to have finished the copying, they were unable to contact me. I returned much later, only to find that for some reason, their machines would process only a few copies of this job. The machines had done other jobs easily. Sighing, I took what had been completed and returned home.

To my dismay and relief, I discovered an error that would have necessitated completely redoing the job. I was able to correct the mistake and return to the shop the next day, where the job was processed easily and quickly. Had I struggled and either demanded they somehow do it or run all over town to different shops, not only would I have been frazzled, but I would have missed a concert and I would have paid for two jobs. Instead, I simply Allowed the circumstance to be what it was and worked with it rather than against it.

When we cease our struggle, we are usually made aware of more options available to us. Scientists tell us that the species that have survived the longest have done so because they are the most adaptive to whatever environment they happen to be in. So it goes with us. We will survive — and thrive — much better when we are at peace and able to see our options sail in over a calm sea.

Otherwise, we contribute to the storms and the resulting shipwrecks.

In Allowing our destiny to unfold, we must remember that it will run in cycles. At some times of our lives, everything we do seems to work. At other times … well, I probably don't have to tell you about *those* times.

Sometimes we feel very creative and full of energy. Other times we may feel like we'd just like to rest for a while and do nothing. Large studies have been done on what is called our circadian cycles, helping us to understand how our energy may surge and fade even during different parts of the day. Each person has his own inner timer which, properly used, can contribute to a healthier, happier life.

The same goes for our work cycles. Some people work steadily, producing day after day, year after year. Others (like me) tend to go in spurts with times of remarkable creativity interspersed with periods of nothing at all. The work habits of most people are somewhere in between.

I now understand that there is no one best way for our cycles to operate. The trick is to find the type of cyclical flow of work and rest that you manage best and refine it.

Once you have discovered your best way of working, don't use it as an excuse to reinforce the weaknesses of it. Instead, become aware of when your particular style is hindering your success and when it contributes to it.

In my case, it is easy to wait until I'm "on a roll" to produce something. In my full life, I always have alternative activities to fill the time allotted to me. However, if I am to fulfill my destiny, I need to bring more discipline into what

I want to accomplish, but not so much that the joy is wrung out of it. If my life is too rigid or scheduled, I tend to begin to go out of whack.

Others tend to like a schedule. It helps them function better. You may find having most of the day organized allows you to function at your best. When you don't have the burden of inventing the day as you proceed, you are freed to be your creative best. It may benefit you to allow more flexibility in your scheduling.

Whatever your particular style, you will discover that there are circumstances when you must work counter to it. Those are the times to remember the practice of Allowance and the giving up of struggle.

Strange as it may seem, there is a benefit to struggling. If you are struggling, you have an excuse not to accomplish your goals. You are able to put on hold the pain that might be caused by changes in your living habits. If you stop struggling, your friends may think you're weird. You will have to give up the negative dramas that spice up your life and keep it interesting. If you start practicing Allowance and start accomplishing more, you might not be able to enjoy the complaining sessions that previously have taken your time. And, what will you do with the extra time?

I know several people, and I'm sure you do too, to whom everything is a drama. It seems as though everything they do must have some sort of dramatic flair to it. This, of course, is one way they get attention. By being rewarded with attention for the drama, they tend to continue it. In my opinion, when everything is a drama, nothing is a drama.

It's much like the boy who cried wolf. When drama becomes tedium, the real problems tend to go unacknowledged and unresolved.

When I'm struggling, my flair for the dramatic emerges. As a speaker, I tell stories to illustrate my points and, of course, these need a certain amount of drama and humor in them. I'm usually poking fun at myself when I tell the stories. But, when I'm living my "real" life, these dramas impede my progress, slowing me down as I Focus on the drama and not my highest good. My life is not enhanced.

Allowance doesn't mean that we Allow our children to grow up morally bankrupt and socially unacceptable. It does mean that we Allow them to grow in the direction of their talents and their particular destinies while we lovingly guide them along the way. It doesn't mean that we just smile when someone is causing us harm. It does mean we Allow those around us their peculiarities which make them individuals. In the practice of Allowance we detach ourselves from our damaging emotions and the poisonous dramas we create. Allowance permits us to take a step back from the show to understand what role we want to play. It means we can Allow our lives and activities to be a little easier.

The following exercise may make you more aware of when you're struggling so you can open more options for yourself.

## *Exercise 15:*

## *Letting Go of Struggle*

To help you gain awareness of where you are struggling, write the answers to the following questions in your notebook:

1.   In what areas of your life do you tend to struggle the most?
2.   What are you struggling with right now?
3.   How does this struggle hinder your life?
4.   What sort of dramas do you play out when you're struggling?
5.   What is the payoff in your life for struggling?
6.   What are the steps I could take this week to practice Allowance?

Watch yourself during the coming week as you practice Allowance by giving up struggle. Make notes about where you catch yourself and where you create drama either to bolster yourself or to get attention. The more you become aware of it, the easier it becomes to Allow that which needs to be allowed and to peacefully change that which must be changed.

℘   ℘   ℘

By Allowing ourselves to be a part of the ebb and flow of life, we become a synchronous part of the universal harmony. We become like a willow tree in a wind storm, bending with the weather, but always returning upright to carry out our destiny in beauty and dignity.

*Chapter 7*

*Focus*

I once heard an interview with the great middle distance runner, Mary Decker Slaney. She was asked how she was able to win so consistently and over a period of so many years. She replied, "Aside from the training, I think it's because I'm able to concentrate on the race longer than the others."

That statement has stayed with me and has become an important part of my own journey in destiny.

On another occasion, I was watching the introductory sequence to Monday-night football several years ago. One clip featured a close-up of the Seahawk's wide receiver, Steve Largent, as he was about to catch a pass. The intensity of Focus registered in his eyes as he zeroed in on the ball was unlike anything I had ever seen. A 280-pound linebacker was lurking on his right, ready to mash him, but Largent held his Intention to catch the ball with a laser-like Focus and was successful. I told my husband, "If I could

Focus like that for even thirty seconds, I could probably rule the world!"

The ability to Focus, even for short periods of time, is one practice that most people in this country sadly lack. However, when we are able to Focus on a single item, our world will change. If we can Focus on something longer, the universe will respond unequivocally.

According to four-time Olympian and motivational coach, Lyle Nelson, the ability to Focus can be learned. It is a mindful skill.

If you are to fulfill your Destiny — in fact, if you are to even remember what it is — you must develop the ability to Focus.

When Jesus performed his miracles, he not only understood that he must work with energy and he must believe what he was doing, he also had to Focus exclusively on what he was doing. When he changed the water to wine, he was not thinking about how he was going to lecture on the hillside. When he raised Lazarus from the dead, he was not concerned with his death on the cross. He concentrated only on what was before him.

When we Focus, it is like tuning into our favorite radio station. We simply don't hear the other frequencies. When Steve Largent Focused on catching the football, for a split second the defensive lineman did not exist, even though he made himself painfully obvious soon thereafter.

When you were asked to gaze at the candle and make it change colors, you were not only engaging in an exercise of Visualization, you were working on developing the ability to Focus. If you are to see the energy fields emitted by your or another's body, you must be able to Focus on that happening.

In fact, if you were to Focus more fully on the tasks you perform at your job or at home, especially those you are not fond of, you would find yourself completing them in far less time, leaving you more time to engage in that which gives you pleasure.

Shortly after I saw the interview with Mary Slaney, I participated in a five kilometer (3.1 miles) fun run. Acting on her cue, I did my best to concentrate on every step I took, how I moved my arms, my posture and my pace and to not think about anything but how I was running for the duration of the race.

First, I found how much work it was. My brain was more fatigued at the end of it than was my body. Obviously, my Focus-er was out of shape!

Second, I discovered that I had run the best race of my life to that date. During that time I had not been consciously trying to beat anyone nor had I been trying to run my best. I had been trying only to Focus.

Have you ever watched a child intent on learning something new? Nothing else exists in her world.

In our world of sound-bites and instant gratification, the ability to Focus may be an endangered species. We need to establish a program to bring back this fading art. So let's start with us.

Learning to Focus takes some work, just as the other eleven Practices do. But the rewards far outpace the dedication required to improve your skill. A friend of mine once journeyed to France, where he stayed for several months.

He said that, although he spoke French when he arrived, having to Focus on understanding it all day left him exhausted for the first few days. He was not used to concentrating for that long.

You, too, may find as did he and I, that initially, Focusing for long periods of time may leave you somewhat fatigued. But, as you develop your Focusing "muscles," you will find it easier and easier to Focus on that which needs to be done.

## *Exercise 16:*

### *Review*

Review the exercises outlined so far in the book. Practice each one again, seeing if you can Focus more intently on its completion. Have as your Intention, not necessarily the perfect accomplishment of the exercise, but your total Focus on the exercise itself.

Become so much a part of the meditations that for that time, nothing else exists in your world. When you write your Ten-Minute Drills, Focus for the entire ten minutes on the question you are answering. Think of nothing else. As you work with your energy ball, become totally immersed in it. The same goes for your six-month projection.

Notice how different the experiences are. Record your observations in your notebook.

## Exercise 17:
## Daily Focus

For the next week pay special attention to the tasks you perform as you go through your day. When you begin a task, think of nothing else. Begin with something simple, such as washing the dishes. As you wash a dish, Focus on it entirely, noticing the pattern, the feel of it when it's soapy, the noise your finger makes as it squeaks across the freshly rinsed surface. The simpler the task, the more obvious the Focus becomes. Of course, you don't need to go through the rest of your life with total Focus while putting on your socks, but it's a good place to start applying the Focus.

ৡ   ৡ   ৡ

Few people know that in addition to being a great comedienne, Lucille Ball was also a savvy business person. She once said that the best advice she ever got was to do what she was doing totally and completely and then move on to the next thing. She added that she had previously tried to think of everything at once and was, of course, scattered in her actions and in her results. But, when she began to Focus on one thing at a time, even if it was just for a couple of minutes, her ability to do the many things on her agenda increased dramatically.

In my own experience this works magnificently. When I forget it, things tend to remain undone and my life gets very scattered. This is one reason I write down what I need to accomplish. If I list all my obligations in a single place, I don't need to use that part of my brain and that energy to remember it all. I can select the next task and Focus on its successful completion to the exclusion of everything else, knowing that, when it's complete, I can return to the list and select my next task. If you have a lot to do, try this method. If you are interrupted in your task, stop and Focus completely on the person who interrupted you, then return immediately to Focusing on your task. If you have to, write down anything you need to remember so you don't have to think about it until you return to your list.

If you are in a place with a lot of noise and distractions, at least for the short term, look upon it as a laboratory in which you can practice Focus. Often, when I am writing or studying, I will purposely go to a busy place where I can sit at my own table. Due to the distractions around me I am forced to totally Focus upon what I'm doing, so that it literally becomes my whole world. I get an amazing amount of work done!

## *Exercise 18*
### *Daily Focus II*

Write the word "Focus" in large letters on at least five index cards. Place a card where you are bound to see it during the week — on your mirror, by your computer, on your desk, in your car and in your daily planner.

Write about your experiences in your Destiny notebook.

ৡ   ৡ   ৡ

As with any other skill, the more you practice, the better you get. I have found that practicing Tai Chi is a wonderful method for developing the ability to Focus. Doing its slow, precise movements correctly takes complete concentration. Deceptively simple, Tai Chi also enhances your ability to breathe and move. I find that, as I Focus on moving through the routine, my mind is actually clearer for several hours and I am better able to Focus on what I am doing during that time. Tai Chi is now widely taught, so you should have no problem locating a class near you.

Here are a some more simple exercises you can do to help you increase your ability to Focus:

## *Exercise 19*

### *Breathing*

Set your timer for two minutes. For those two minutes, watch yourself breathe. Focus on nothing else but your breath. Notice how it sounds and how your body feels with each inhalation and exhalation. Become aware of how deeply you breathe and from where your breath comes. If your mind wanders, reset your timer for two minutes and begin again. Repeat this exercise until you can Focus totally on your breath for two minutes. Continue to Focus on your breath for two minutes each day for a week. When you master two minutes, increase it by a minute. Each time you master the increased time, add one more minute until you reach ten minutes. When you are able to Focus totally on your breath for ten minutes each day for a week, go on to the next exercise.

## *Exercise 20:*
### *Breath and Body*

While walking, begin to Focus on your breath as you did in the above exercise. While Focusing on your breath, become aware of your body. Still Focusing on your breath, notice how your arms move and how your feet are placed. Observe how your breath interacts with the movements of your body. Continue this as long as you are able to maintain total Focus. If your mind wanders, take a couple deep breaths, walk several steps and begin again. I recommend completing this exercise where traffic is not a problem. I don't want you walking into a moving vehicle! You will discover as you develop the ability to Focus on your body and your breath more and more, your mind will become better able to Focus on that which is at hand. Your problem-solving ability will improve as will your creativity. You will most likely increase your ability to remember facts and details and perceive things more clearly.

Some health practitioners today work with energy as a tool for healing. The nursing profession uses Therapeutic Touch and other such practices. More and more people are learning to use the art of Reiki to help themselves and others achieve optimum health. If you wish to develop the ability to use energy for this purpose, you must develop the skill of Focus. Although I've learned how to apply Reiki and some other techniques, I find that the simplest method to transfer energy is to Focus on my hands prior to touching the other person. I also use this method when easing an ache or pain after a strenuous workout.

## *Exercise 21:*
## *Healing Focus*

The point of this exercise is to develop the ability to focus while engaged in a healing activity. As you perform the exercise, concentrate only on the movement of energy through and out of you, not on the outcome. See if you can become totally immersed in the energy that flows out of your hands.

1. Sit quietly and relax. Take a deep breath through your nose and imagine that you are pulling in healing energy from the universe through the top of your head. Feel it enter as if you had a funnel inserted in your head and the energy rushed into it. As you exhale through your mouth, direct this energy down your arms and into your hands. Repeat the breathing and energy movement until you feel your hands pulsing with energy or receive some other signal that the energy is ready to transfer to the other person.
2. Place your hands close to the area of the person who needs healing. (If you are

uncertain, ask for guidance or simply place your hands on that person's head.) Concentrate on acting as the conduit for the energy and take a deep breath. As you exhale, feel the energy moving through you and out your hands. Focus completely on your hands. Hold the Focus as you continue to breath and move the energy. With practice you will recognize when the exercise is complete. It feels like the energy stops flowing.

You may find your hands becoming warm after you have been Focusing for several minutes. Continue until the warmth subsides. If you feel at all lightheaded, sit down. (It is perfectly fine to remain seated during the entire exercise.)

ॐ   ॐ   ॐ

This may be a short chapter, but don't confuse its length with the importance of this practice. It is the rocket booster, propelling the other practices into the next level.

*Chapter 8*

*Forgiveness*

When I talk about forgiveness, most people groan and say, "I can do everything but forgive _____ (fill in the blank);" or they will say, "If I forgive _____, I will be condoning what that person has done;" *or* they piously say, "Well, I've forgiven everyone, so I don't need to do much work on this."

Forgiveness is a cornerstone of your destiny and must support the structure upon which you build your life. Without complete Forgiveness of everyone, you cannot fully express the life you were sent here to lead. It can be the most gut-wrenching and difficult practice to implement, yet it can also be the most rewarding when you understand and apply it. For some people, it seems as if complete Forgiveness is just too much to ask.

My views on Forgiveness are a little different from what others may consider it to be. During the years I've actively studied it, I've learned a lot about Forgiveness — what it is and what it isn't. In its simplest form, Forgiveness is the practice of removing one's negative energy from something or someone. It can be a little difficult to grasp at first. Because of the reactions I've encountered when talking about Forgiveness, I'm going to start by describing what Forgiveness is not. It is not:

- *Condoning actions which are harmful to self or others.*

  Angie was upset because another woman, Susan, had been spreading a story about her which was not only untrue, but potentially damaging both personally and professionally. She not only wanted Susan to stop the story, she wanted her to apologize and recant publicly. She was gathering evidence for a lawsuit, but didn't want to go that far. After I explained to her the concept of removing her negative energy from the situation, Angie elected to confront Susan in a calm manner and explain to her that she was aware of the activity and that it needed to stop. Since Angie had removed her negative energy from — that is, she forgave — Susan, she was able to not only present her side, but calmly explain to Susan the potential ramifications, including a lawsuit, that could follow. Angie refused to be drawn into an argument and did not become the least bit upset during the entire process. The harmful stories stopped immediately.

By practicing Forgiveness, Angie was able to view the situation objectively and decide on a course of action that not only brought the predicament to a swift resolution, but gave her the courage to eliminate some other negative conditions in her life without creating big disturbances.

- *Staying in the role of "victim."*

    Perry's boss was abusive and over-bearing, causing stress not only to Perry, but to his co-workers as well. When I talked to Perry, he was at his wit's end, afraid to leave the job because he needed the income, yet realizing that he was placing himself in the role of victim. As he worked to remove his negative energy from his plight, he began to see the job in a new light. He realized that he had more options than he had at first realized. With this new-found strength, he quickly secured a position at another firm and not only gained a supportive supervisor, but a raise in salary as well. When Perry removed his negative energy from the situation and began Focusing on other possibilities, they appeared quickly.

- *Shirking civil responsibilities.*

    Some people feel that Forgiveness includes complete non-involvement when harm is being done and is likely to continue. Darlene came home to find her house ransacked and several precious possessions missing. In addition to being agitated about the crime, she felt guilty about reporting it to the police, feeling it was not a Forgiving thing to do. I pointed out that reporting a crime has nothing to do with Forgiveness. When she was able to take a more objective view of the situation, she realized that by reporting it, she was protecting others from harm by aiding in removing the criminals from the streets. Forgiveness is being able to act from a sense of a higher purpose and not from revenge.

- *Enabling another to continue to abuse you.*

Vic had loaned money to his brother on several occasions, but had never been repaid. Vic felt that, as a forgiving person, he needed not only to Forgive his brother each time, but to continue to loan him money. I told Vic that, in essence, he was contributing to his brother's irresponsibility rather than looking at the higher view. The result was ongoing abuse of Vic's good nature by Frank. After completing the forgiveness process, Vic told Frank he would no longer "lend" him money. It took a few incidents in which Vic had to stand his ground, but as he learned to come from his higher nature, he was able to turn his brother down, telling him it was time for both of them to be accountable. The relationship was tense for a while, but Frank finally understood that Vic would no longer play his game. I don't know if Frank has changed, but Vic has and is much happier as a result.

- *Expecting change in the other person.*
  One of my favorite sayings is "Don't expect a tiger to be a giraffe." In other words, people are who they are and will usually behave in the future as they have in the past unless something compelling happens to change them. A tiger will not become a vegetarian just because you forgave it for eating an antelope. I often encounter disappointment from people who tell me, "I forgave _____ for hurting me, but he just went out and did the same thing again!" Perhaps it is unfortunate that people do not change just because we bestow Forgiveness upon them. You must keep in mind that Forgiveness is entirely for your benefit. When you remove your energy from the misdeeds of another, you are actually in a better position to protect yourself from being affected by them again. If you are not expecting a change in the other person, you will not so easily be hurt again.

- *Waiting for the other person to repent, to grant Forgiveness.*

    Have you ever said or thought, "Well, I'll forgive that person just as soon as she apologizes." When you say that, you are not really considering the practice of Forgiveness. You are practicing retribution. I do not teach retribution. You must practice Forgiveness without even involving the other person. As long as you are waiting for the other person to apologize, you are allowing yourself to be controlled by that person. You are not expressing the fullness of who you are.

Once I figured out what Forgiveness is not, I was naturally brought to the point of contemplating what Forgiveness really is. Forgiveness is:

- Removing your impeding emotions from the situation or person,
- Getting on with your life,
- Understanding and eliminating your own fears in the situation.

Forgiveness tells you and the world more about you than about the other person. In other words, when you forgive someone:

- What that person did tells the world about him or her.

- How you forgive tells the world about you.

A woman came to me to talk about her troubled marriage. Her husband found fault with everything she did, from the way she dressed to the way she disciplined their children. This had gone on for many years. By the time she came to see me, she was a combination of defeat, anger and frustration. "I've forgiven him and forgiven him," she said, "but he doesn't think he does anything wrong. Maybe he's right. Maybe I am just a terrible wife, mother and person. But it hurts so much when he says those things. I just don't know what to do."

As we talked, I helped her to see that her husband's criticisms were a reflection of his own sense of lack and reflected his own fears. She realized that she needed to see her own worth. In her case, Forgiveness entailed ceasing to accept his criticisms and drawing on her own strength and self-worth. The next time he criticized her, she calmly replied, "That's not true. I no longer accept that about myself and will no longer listen to it from you." And she left the room.

It took a lot of dedication on her part, but slowly, the couple were able to resolve the issue of his criticism. They sought counseling. He recognized how his fears as well as his upbringing contributed to his behavior, and she was able to see how her fears had added to his behavior over the years. Last I heard, they were both doing well, but nothing happened until she realized that his behavior was about him and had nothing to do with her.

By the same token, our willingness and ability to forgive another person tells us and the world about our character. Most of the reactions we have toward other people are caused by our own fears, beliefs and conditioning over the years. Later in this chapter is an exercise to help you get to the root cause of these fears and help you to triumph in Forgiveness.

One dear woman to whom I was explaining this concept got very upset with me when I told her that her anger toward a certain gentleman was not about what he had done, but about her own fears and hurts. "That means that I'm wrong and he's right," she insisted. I'm not sure I ever was able to explain the concept to her in terms that would help her to see that the person who was really being hurt by her bitter and unforgiving attitude was herself, not the one who purportedly did the terrible deed. Unfortunately, she remains bitter to this day and it pervades her whole life.

Holding a grudge or unforgiving attitude seems to have a payoff. After all, if we hold tight to that ill feeling, we don't have to look deeper within ourselves and face the fear that is causing us to react as we do. It means we can be right and the other person wrong. Releasing negative energy from a situation isn't as dramatic as re-telling the story of how so and so "done us wrong." Unfortunately, it also holds us back from living in freedom.

Jesus said that we should never pray when we are holding anything at all against another. This is a tall order! However, Jesus knew that if we hold something in our heart which is not loving of another, we adulterate the energy of our prayer and it becomes less effective. Are you catching on to the idea of how practical this ancient advice is?

Understanding the practical nature of Forgiveness is important when fulfilling your destiny. Your good and your destiny cannot unfold and flow through a heart congested with unforgiveness. Not only that, Forgiveness is one of those actions which releases endorphins and other healing chemicals into our systems. Believe me, the ancient mystics knew what they were talking about!

Whom does unforgiveness hurt the most? Believe it or not, it's the person holding the unforgiving feelings. Isn't it strange how we seek to punish someone by not forgiving them and end up harming ourselves the most? When we harbor harsh condemnations, we literally dump poisons into our bodies. Many cancers or cases of arthritis and heart disease can be traced directly to long-term unresolved anger and unforgiving attitudes. So, first of all, explore where you are unloving toward yourself.

Whether to forgive or not can become a habit. If you consciously adopt the habit of Forgiveness, this does not mean that you will be spared being hurt. However, by forgiving you can move through harmful feelings faster, take the necessary, empowering action, and get on with your life.

Here's an example of what can happen when, instead of nurturing and caring for your hurt, you move through it and empower yourself to wholeness.

A colleague and his wife occasionally engaged in picking at each other — as happens in relationships. He realized that one type of comment his wife habitually made was rather abusive, causing him to counter with his own form of verbal abuse and ultimately resulting in his being upset for days. One day he decided he didn't want his "buttons" pushed by her remarks any longer and would forgive her (remove his energy from the situation). The next time she made an abrasive comment, he looked lovingly at his wife and said, "This feels abusive to me and I don't want to listen to it." At that point he smiled sweetly, got up and walked out of the room.

His wife was left standing alone with no one to play the game. After it happened a couple more times, she realized he had removed his energy from this circumstance, and she quit making annoying remarks. Fortunately, she was intelligent and loving enough to understand what had happened, and the couple was able to explore a healthier approach to their discussions.

Do you remember Marley's ghost in Dickens' story, *A Christmas Carol?* He was forced to drag the chains of his misdeeds through all eternity. At the beginning of the story, he tried to warn Ebeneezer Scrooge about the same fate awaiting him. I remember watching the movie as a child and wondering what I might be doing to build a chain that would drag me down. At the time I was a little more concerned about eternity than about my life (give me a break—I was only seven!), but the image has stayed with me. I now know how heavy those chains can become in this life.

I once took a class in prosperity. One of the lessons — that of Forgiveness — turned into a two-year project involving forgiving and releasing people and hurts. I found out that, even though I thought of myself as a forgiving person, I carried a lot of sludge inside. And at first I thought, "Oh, I've forgiven everyone." That was my first rude awakening. The second, even ruder awakening, was discovering how much energy these stuffed emotions drained from me. The toll was way too expensive.

I also noticed something else as I began to forgive and release — my life got easier. I'm certainly not going to tell you that my problems disappeared. I found, however, that moving through them was so much easier when I didn't have all those chains dragging me down!

The highest form of Forgiveness, to paraphrase a concept from *A Course In Miracles,* is to realize that what we thought someone else had done to us never really happened. This is certainly a worthy aspiration, but perhaps not the best place to start. If you are already there, congratulations. However, for us mere mortals, let's look at a step-by-step approach that will at least get us to peace of mind and heal relationships.

First of all, don't worry about the anger, hurt and even hatred you currently feel toward someone. In fact, acknowledging these feelings is the first step to Forgiveness. This step is difficult in itself, since we must face the rather unattractive darkness that lurks in all of us. This step requires a lot of courage. Forgiveness is not for sissies. So, if you'd rather remain a victim, you may wish to go on to other chapters and come back to this one when you're ready.

If you have decided to go ahead, let's explore Forgiveness a little further.

In Leviticus 16:9-10, Aaron is told to bundle up his sins, put them on the back of a goat (the scapegoat) and then send the goat into the wilderness. Most of us bundle up our hurts and fears, and tie them on the back of a

**Your Scapegoat**

convenient target. Then, instead of sending the bundle into the wilderness, we strap it to our own backs and drag it around. Frankly, carrying the smelly, old goat of unforgiveness around is not something that appeals to me. Let it go!

## *Exercise 22:*
## *The Scapegoat*

Make ten copies of the picture of the goat on the facing page. On one copy, write down all the hurts, old stuff, grudges and anger that you hold toward others. Write down everything you can think of that you need to forgive someone for, even if you don't feel they deserve it, and even if you don't want to forgive that person. Once you feel complete, burn the paper. If you have no safe receptacle, tear the page into tiny bits and take them outside to the garbage. Once you start this exercise don't go on to something else until you have burned the paper. This is why you need to make several copies of the picture. Each time you come back to the exercise, start with a fresh goat. You may find yourself writing the same grudge or hurt each time. Don't get discouraged if this is the case. I once worked consistently for two years on forgiving a certain person. And, after that, intermittently for about five more years.

Using the image of the goat can also come in handy for new incidents. The next time someone hurts your feelings, just picture him riding into the sunset on a goat. It may not change him, but it will probably make you feel better. (And the other guy will wonder what you're smiling at when he's trying to insult you!)

Sometimes it's important to let an individual know how his or her behavior is affecting you, especially if you must regularly spend time in the presence of that person. I've realized that, even though I know that my hurts are about me, I'm not always emotionally ready to deal with it. I try to tell the other person how the action is affecting me without making him wrong. This can be tricky, especially since our society is so right-and-wrong oriented. I have found that, even putting it in the context of, "This is about me," I often encounter resistance because the other person feels criticized. If that happens, don't get upset or hooked into an argument. Just remain calm while the individual reacts. Then, thank that person for hearing you out and leave.

I usually say something like, "This is not about anything you've done that's wrong, but I'd like to tell you how I tend to react when you say _____. Because I don't seem to be able to deal with it — again, this is about me, not about you — could you help me out by _____?"

It usually takes a little up-front planning, but can be very effective if the person is truly interested in working on the relationship. If the other person is not interested in working on the relationship, heal yourself and move on.

Sometimes you need to seek competent professional help in resolving issues. This is not something to be ashamed of. If it gets you through, by all means, seek help. Let your counselor know, that you are not seeking to stay in blame, but are looking to get healthy.

Here is a good exercise to get you started in eliminating blame from your life.

## *Exercise 23:*
## *Ten-Minute Drill — Blame*

As you write in your notebook for ten minutes without stopping, answer the following question:

What if no one were to blame?

After you've finished, re-read what you've just written. Highlight or circle those phrases or sentences which have an impact on you. This exercise will help you to see what role blame is playing in your life and may give you some ideas about how you might shift your thinking and behavior to eliminate spending your energy on this destructive behavior.

You may need to talk with the other person about how you are being affected, but do not do so until you are sure of the real reason behind your feelings so that you don't disintegrate into a blaming war. If you are troubled with that, write for another ten minutes, answering the question, "What if no one were wrong?" This has helped many people resolve relationship issues.

## Exercise 24:
## Getting To The Root

Have you ever been so hurt or angry that you didn't want to forgive someone? Or, have you been in the position where you want to let go of the negative emotions, but can't seem to do so? Those feelings can be pretty persistent, hanging on like a second skin. Peeling them off is not easy. It often takes getting to the root of the fears which cause them to cling. Understanding what is at the root of your feelings may help you get to the point where you are able to let go of them. Some of us discover that the real reason we cant or won't forgive is different from the reason we think at first.

This exercise may help you resolve some feelings that won't go away easily.

Complete the following statements in your notebook:

- I haven't forgiven _____ because:
- My payoff for unforgiveness is:
- I am choosing to forgive _____ because (this should describe a benefit to you for forgiving this person):
- My fear about this is:
- I have this fear because:
- If I release this fear:

You know when you've gotten to the root when the other person is no longer a part of the equation. When you stand alone with the fear, it usually means you have arrived at the real reason for your unforgiving feelings.

When Denise came to see me, she was simply unable to forgive a co-worker for having engaged in unethical behavior to get a promotion for which Denise was in line. Denise had tried for months to work through her feelings of anger, but to no avail. Her progress through the above exercise ended up something like this. (I have greatly simplified it.)

"I haven't forgiven Emily because her lies about me resulted in my not getting the promotion I was promised. The payoff to me is that I have an excuse for no longer working as hard or as enthusiastically as I used to. I am choosing to forgive Emily because my ability to work effectively and enjoy my job has been seriously compromised by my feelings. My fear is, if I forgive her, she may step on me again. I have this fear because, if I allow people to step on me, I may never get promoted. If I release this fear, I not only can work to the highest of my ability, not worrying about others, but I may be open to even greater job prospects."

As Denise reviewed her fears, she realized that she was in a sense allowing Emily to rule her emotions. Her fear that Emily would do it again (which was quite likely) plus her apprehension about never receiving a promotion were keeping her from performing at her best. And, she was getting to the point where she hated going to work. Although it took a few weeks of concentrated effort understanding that her real fear was that she might never move ahead, she was able to recapture her old enthusiasm and productivity at her job. She released the fears about her status and vowed to just do the best job she could. In the end she secured a position that was far superior to the one for which she was passed up. And, Emily was no longer a part of her world.

Emily didn't change. Denise did. And, as a result, her world also changed.

You may need to talk with the other person about how you are being affected, but do not do so until you are sure of the real reason behind your feelings so that you don't disintegrate into a blaming war. If you are having trouble with that, write for another ten minutes, answering the question, "What if I no longer needed to defend my point of view?" This has helped many people resolve relationship issues.

ఴ  ఴ  ఴ

As I mentioned before, I once embarked on a two-year odyssey of forgiveness. To tell you the truth, I was happy when that time was over. However, not only did I learn a lot about myself, but by the end of the year I felt much freer from the burdens of the past. An affirmation I used often was:

> *I fully and freely forgive and release everyone who I think harmed (insulted, hurt, etc.) me ."*

This had an interesting, although somewhat alarming, effect. To the surface would bubble all the feelings about people I had held for years. I remembered incidents which now seemed so trivial that I couldn't believe they were still a part of my anger. I would get angry all over again. And the longer I stayed incensed, the more often these ghosts would surface to haunt me.

One night I suddenly realized that these incidents were making themselves known to me so they could pass out of my body and out of my consciousness. At that point I began to welcome them. I reviewed them to understand why they still bothered me then bid them farewell. From that day on I was rarely revisited by my long-dead "friends."

This phenomenon was explained to me several years later. The person told me that when we take a stand to grow to a higher level, everything that is unlike the person we are becoming must leave to make room for the new. In my case, everything that was like unforgiveness was doing its best to leave me to make room for a fresh, more loving me.

Sometimes it helps to have an imaginary conversation with someone. Tell that person or write that person a letter outlining all the hurts and ills that person caused you. After you have finished, go back and highlight each one. Then go through the previous exercise, discovering what you fear in each step. This process often helps to begin to resolve old wounds and heal old relationships.

Does forgiving someone mean you let an abusive spouse back in your life? Does it mean you continue to "loan" money to someone who never pays you back? Does it mean you keep on working for a boss who belittles you or a company that has demeaning practices? Does it mean you never tell your truth? I used to think it did, but that's not true. Does it mean you continue to support a lazy adult child who won't take responsibility?

Of course not. It means that you have a clear picture of who you are and what you need. It means you can walk away from a situation without carrying the burden of hatred with you. It means you can act from the highest possible solution because you are not mired down in the swamp of victimization.

You cannot resolve hatred with an unforgiving heart. You cannot act with courage if you are cowering in a corner, whimpering, "Poor me."

Forgiving can at first feel like surgery to have a body part removed. A phenomenon among amputees is the "ghost limb" syndrome, where the patient feels pain in a limb or organ that no longer exists. At first, we may miss the old familiar hate. After all, it's such a convenient place to put those fears we are hiding from. But, gradually, we get used to the idea of Forgiveness and actually begin to feel more energetic, even healed.

I have noticed a trend lately to which we should pay attention. We are certainly aware that some people do terrible things to others. I, too, know the heartbreak of losing a family member at the hand of another. In one high-profile case, the father of a murder victim consistently says, "I'm just looking for justice." However, his behavior and demeanor says that he is looking for revenge. In his quest for the destruction of another person, he long ago lost sight of justice.

In fact, I long ago stopped asking for justice in my life. I quit asking for what I deserve. Frankly, I don't know what I deserve and I'm not entirely sure what justice looks like in the eyes of God. I do, however, ask for grace. In its simplest form, grace is clemency. I realize that I cannot, no matter how hard I try, live a perfect life. I will unknowingly hurt others and fall short of the mark. So, when others hurt you, rather than seeking justice and retribution, seek first grace. Then proceed from there.

More often than not, Forgiveness really does heal relationships. The strange thing is that we often need do nothing other than forgive and release the other person. In one case, a young woman was estranged from her father because of an argument they had had several years earlier. She realized that she needed to forgive both of them (and especially herself for holding such unresolved resentment). She began sending loving thoughts through herself to him. After a few days of this, her father called and they immediately began the healing. Soon it was as if the incident had never happened. Think how many years they lost just because of some petty hurts!

I recently listened to an interview with the great golf pro, Greg Norman, as he discussed how he handled his last-day collapse at the 1996 U.S. Masters Tournament, one of the most prestigious tournament in the golf world. After leading by a wide margin the first three days, he shot a six over par 78 on Sunday, losing the tournament to Nick Price, a seemingly crushing defeat.

The interviewer asked him how he handled the loss. Norman replied that he asked himself what a loving father would tell his son if the son returned home, defeated and broken. Greg thought a loving, supportive father might say: "Congratulations! You played a terrific series and took second at the most prestigious tournament in the country. Remember, golf is just a game and you're a wonderful person. It's in the past now and there will be another tournament tomorrow."

Then, Greg Norman repeated these uplifting words to himself and prepared for his next tournament.

What if we treated ourselves in the same manner as a loving father or mother or friend? What would we say to ourselves if we suffered a defeat or felt like a failure? Forgiveness entails forgiving ourselves first. Go back to exercise titled "Getting To The Root." Insert your own name in the first sentence and complete the exercise. By treating yourself as a person who is worthy of being forgiven, you will find it much easier to forgive others. As we seek grace, we realize that mercy extends to us, no matter what we have done.

As you step out in a new way, remember what Jesus said to the woman at the well, "Your sins are forgiven. Go and sin no more." Begin now. If you have harmed another, do the best you can to make amends. This includes forgiving yourself for not forgiving others. Then as Jesus commanded, sin no more. In other words, don't repeat what you have done.

When someone hurts you or something upsets you, let your thoughts turn as early as possible to, "How can I forgive this?" As soon as you can forgive, you can solve the problem. Forgive yourself. Forgive others. You will walk with a new lilt to your step and a fresh smile on your face.

How often do I work on forgiveness? Every day. Do I like It? Not usually. Do I like the results? Always.

*Chapter 9*

*Discipline*

I can almost hear a collective groan when I introduce this practice. "I just can't stick with it," seems to be the mantra of many people today. And, no wonder! Most of our lives are so fast-paced that just fitting in what seems to be the minimum amount is tough enough. How are we supposed to Discipline ourselves to remember and fulfill our destiny, too?

It may not be as tough as it seems. It's obvious that, if you are to adopt the practices in this book, even on a very limited scale, and set forth on the path of remembering, applying, and fulfilling your destiny, you need some sort of Discipline to keep you Focused on that path.

Chances are you are already practicing an enormous amount of Discipline in your life. You get up each morning and go to work. You care for your family and friends. You eat every day and practice good hygiene. You wear clean clothes and keep your living area suitable for habitation (although my office is not always a good example). If you are doing these things, you are already practicing enough Discipline to survive in today's society.

When I speak about Discipline as one of the Twelve Practices, I am referring to what I call "Directed Discipline." This is the Discipline necessary to move out of simply getting by, day to day. It is the practice we must engage in to move ourselves beyond existence and into living abundantly and joyfully.

If you are to acquire even a modicum of skill in any of the Practices, you must be disciplined enough to do them daily for a few minutes. You must be disciplined enough to make time in your day to apply them.

One reason the practice of Discipline has been placed late in the book instead of early is that it's very difficult to practice Discipline without understanding why.

For example, if you are in the habit of drinking several cups of coffee every day and are told that you need to quit drinking it, unless you understood why, you probably would not go through the withdrawal necessary without a good reason.

The same goes for Discipline. Unless you could understand that your life would improve dramatically just by introducing Directed Discipline into it, you might not adopt it as a practice.

When we practice Discipline, we lay aside a temporary pleasure for a long-term result. If you are not willing to do this, you will not fulfill your destiny.

Behind Discipline is a well-placed Intention. You must first set and hold an Intention to accomplish something. You must then acquire the Discipline necessary to complete it.

All this may seem obvious to you. However, as we each examine our lives, we realize that, even though we are disciplined enough to get through each day, pockets of our lives no doubt need attention in this area.

I have had the sad experience of knowing people who, because of their smoking, developed cancer. Even to save their lives, they elected not to develop the Discipline to shed the habit.

I knew a woman who constantly commented about how fit I was and how healthy I was. She would say things like, "I wish I had a body like yours. I wish I was so slim and trim. You're so lucky." I finally could take no more and in the nicest manner I could muster, I said, "You *can* be slim and trim like me. You have the ability to do it. All you have to do is Discipline yourself to eat healthy foods and run thirty miles a week. But, you have to be willing to pay the price. Otherwise, you are really saying that you don't want it because you've not made the decision to be Disciplined."

She hid her chocolate bar behind her back and shrugged. "I just can't seem to stick with it," she said. "I'm so busy, you know."

"We all are," I gently replied. "I guess we're just disciplined in those areas that are the most important to us. My health is important to me, so I Focus on that and make the time for it."

It's a shame that Discipline as a subject isn't taught in more schools. If, as children, we learned more about the benefits of becoming disciplined about our habits, we would, no doubt, have an easier time of it. Many of us were told that we had to study during certain hours or practice piano for a certain length of time. I wasn't always sure why, except that it seemed to make everyone happier when I complied. And, I always felt good when my grades were high. It wasn't until later in life that I really connected Discipline to the health of my mind, body, and spirit.

Discipline has never come to me naturally. As with Visualization or Access, some people have a more natural talent or disposition for it. However, like the other Practices, Discipline can be developed to a high degree, even though it may not be your natural bent. In working on my own discipline, I have watched the pendulum swing from one extreme to the other. For a time, I was so Disciplined that I became rigid. Anything that threatened to impose on my carefully laid out days and plans threw me into a tailspin. I actually accomplished an incredible amount of work, but little of it was satisfying, and the result was a deteriorating physical condition due to stress and burn-out. After that the pendulum swung to the other extreme. I lived totally in the moment with no Discipline whatsoever. Fortunately, that phase was short-lived as I discovered that mode of living didn't suit me either.

I have found for myself a sort of middle ground, with plenty of room for the unstructured times I need to take care of my need to play and to handle all those things which are not in my schedule, but with enough Discipline built in so that I regularly work out, get my work done, eat well, and spend vital time on spiritual growth.

As with most people, I lead a very busy life and have a great deal of responsibility. This has created the necessity to carefully examine my activities to make sure that they fit into my destiny. Examining your activities can uncover where you can increase your Discipline and create the time you need to manifest your destiny.

Are you creating busy-ness? I discovered this concept quite by accident when I noticed that I had a pattern of setting a lofty goal, then immediately taking on so much responsibility that there was no way I could possibly achieve the goal. The payoff for doing this was that I didn't have to face possible failure associated with the goal. It could remain a dream. After all, I was far too busy to go after it now.

When I began to examine which activities were contributing to fulfilling my destiny and which were impeding its manifestation, I realized how much I had been creating busy-ness. I eliminated several activities, including those which had once served my journey, but which were no longer appropriate to its expression.

To practice Discipline, you must first decide where in your life more Discipline is needed. Sometimes you may find that, as you become disciplined in one area of your life, another area sort of falls apart. You must then pay attention to that. And so on. Each time you complete a "round" of Discipline in your life, you will find that, overall, its quality has improved. You may find yourself eliminating habits that once served you.

As with the other practices, start with something simple. If you decide that, after a sedentary life, you will suddenly exercise for forty-five minutes a day, you may fall back on your old habits very soon. It will be too difficult and your muscles will be too sore. I see the results of this each year at the gym where I lift weights. In January the gym is so packed that sometimes we have to wait for a machine to open up. In February, although the machines are fairly full, there's rarely a wait. By March, I can pick any machine at random, because most of the people have left their Intentions and their Discipline somewhere in the steam room.

But, what if you decide to practice Discipline by joining a beginning exercise class that meets three times a week for an hour? You will be with others at approximately your fitness level who will encourage you to continue with your resolution. And, these classes are usually enjoyable, contributing to your resolution to continue.

When you have adopted the exercise class as an integral part of your life, you may wish to make a change in your diet. Perhaps you want to eliminate caffeine from your life. Start by cutting back on the amount of coffee you drink. Or, mix your coffee with half decaffeinated and half regular. You decide what's best for you. If we make a one percent change in our habits each day, by the end of a year, life will seem no more difficult, but it will have changed dramatically in its outpicturing.

Use this exercise to help get you started on a more disciplined life:

## *Exercise 25:*
## *Ten Minute Drill — Discipline*

Write in your notebook for ten minutes without stopping, answering this question: "How would my life change for the better if I were more disciplined?"

When you have finished writing, go back and read it. Highlight or underline statements which seem important to you.

Select one area in your life, such as physical health or spiritual practice, that you would like to change. For instance, you may find it easy to skip morning meditation or setting Intentions, but want to develop the Discipline to incorporate them into your life..

Decide on one small action that you could take each day for the next week that you can easily accomplish, but which will require attention to Discipline. You may decide that you will meditate for one minute each morning. This may seem so insignificant that you wonder why you should even bother. However, Discipline comes from consistency and persistence more than from making one great effort. If you meditate for two hours each day, but continue it for only one day, it will not do you as much good as if you were to sit in the silence for one minute a day for the next twenty years.

When you have selected the area of Discipline you will Focus on for the next week, write an Intention to do so. Your Intention might read, "It is my Intention to eat three servings of vegetables each day."

Next, make up some sort of chart, where you track your Discipline. It might be very simple, such as a checklist with your Intention at the top and the days of the week listed below, with a line by each to check off. It probably looks something like this:

My Intention: Walk fifteen minutes each day.

\_\_\_\_\_ Sunday
\_\_\_\_\_ Monday
\_\_\_\_\_ Tuesday
\_\_\_\_\_ Wednesday
\_\_\_\_\_ Thursday
\_\_\_\_\_ Friday
\_\_\_\_\_ Saturday

When you complete your Intention for the day, just check it off.

When I wrote my first book, I wanted to complete it in a certain number of days. I had everything I needed to write it, but I was creating busy-ness everywhere to avoid it. My house had never been cleaner! I finally decided to be more Disciplined about the book. I determined when I wanted to finish the first draft. I divided the anticipated number of words the book would contain by the number of days I had left before my self-imposed deadline and calculated how many words I would write each day. At the end of the first day, when I had written the requisite number of words, I started a bar graph, showing how many words I wrote each day and the cumulative total. At the end of each day, I printed a new chart adding a bar for the day's progress and a line showing the cumulative work to date. I then posted the chart in a prominent place. Because I put it on paper and made myself look at it each day, it took me only a few days to achieve the necessary Discipline to complete my book in the time I had allowed.

It may help you to enlist the aid of a friend when developing your practice of Discipline. Some of my colleagues and I have agreed to give each other motivational kicks when we want to accomplish something, but keep putting it off. We absolutely refuse to accept the others' excuses. Find someone who wants to accomplish a goal that will take Discipline and agree with that person that you will be accountable to each other. Be tough with each other and stay with it.

Enroll in a class to help you advance. I've found that there's nothing like a regularly scheduled event to keep us on track. I practice piano much more consistently when I have a lesson scheduled. And, of course, I am always happy when I practice because I enjoy the playing so much more. Do whatever it takes to get yourself on a regular practice of Discipline.

When you've finished your first week of taking a small step, add something else. Keep building on your successes and get up and keep going when you fall down. Discipline is a matter of (from now on) keeping on.

*Chapter 10*

*Congruence*

A recent study concerning television use in hotels found that requests for pornographic "pay-per-view" movies soared during Christian conferences. A parent lectures his child on the evils of drugs use, then lights a cigarette and drinks a beer. A family court judge is arrested for beating his wife.

These are examples of people living incongruently. And, if we are to realize our destiny, we must begin to practice Congruence.

Congruence is the practice of living in a manner that supports your beliefs. This is a subtle area, but one in which most of us get caught. Very few people — none that I've met so far — live totally in accordance with what they think they believe.

Yet, most of us live according to what we believe deep inside and that's what creates conflict in our lives.

For instance, if I say I believe that I should live in a healthy manner, yet at the same time eat sweets, then what

I am really saying is that I know I should eat healthy foods, but something in my core belief is different from the behavior I am demonstrating.

If, in your professed system of beliefs, you say that you have faith in God, but turn around and worry about something, you have just stepped out of Congruence. A person cannot have faith and worry at the same time. Rather than affirm your faith, you have affirmed that you believe in some other power. Otherwise, you wouldn't worry.

So, what has happened? Even though you say you believe in God's power, something deep inside you isn't truly convinced of the fact. That part of you, the deep-down part, decides what you really believe. And, you don't always know what it is. This is why we continue to manifest the apparent paradox between what we say we believe and how we act.

The practice of Congruence will help you to identify where your core beliefs and your professed beliefs differ. It will also help you bring your core beliefs into line with what you profess to believe.

The first step is to identify your core beliefs that are in conflict with your stated beliefs. It will help you determine whether you want to change the belief or the behavior. You might even find that you want to change both. After all, you will bring into your life that which is in accordance with what you believe.

When I wrote my first book, I found that, at a certain point, I was blocked. I knew what I was going to write, so it wasn't writer's block, but I simply couldn't seem to bring myself to do it. After several weeks of frustration, I finally asked myself, "Okay, what's going on?"

My answer was that I didn't really believe anyone would buy the book (so why put out the effort?). That belief at the time was stronger than the one I kept telling myself: that people *would* buy it. Once I resolved the core belief and got it into Congruence with my professed belief, I easily finished the book and it was published. It has proven to be very popular.

Every core belief we consciously or unconsciously hold has a "behavioral conclusion" that goes along with it. That belief will cause some action on our part to bring us into alignment with the core belief.

This may be why, when I say I can easily lose five pounds, I immediately want a pizza. Something inside of me doesn't believe I can actually do it. If I am to lose and keep off the five pounds, I need to change the inner belief or it will never happen.

To help you understand more about your core beliefs versus your professed beliefs and the resulting action, complete the exercise below.

## *Exercise 26:*
## *Core Beliefs*

In your Destiny Journal write four general beliefs that you hold, such as "I believe in telling the truth." Then, write a "behavioral conclusion" to each, such as (continuing the example) "therefore, I don't stuff my truth." Continue your sentence with the "however." For instance, "however, I often withhold my truth." Then, finish the sentence with the "because:" "because I'm afraid of what someone else might think."

Worksheet:

I believe:
Therefore:
However:
Because:

Some samples of beliefs:

- Love
- Brotherhood
- Health
- Equality
- Freedom

Examples of "therefores:"

- I act boldly on what I am guided to do
- I make the phone calls I need to make
- I eat only the most wholesome foods
- I tell my truth without making the other person wrong

Examples of "howevers:"

- I often withhold my truth
- I postpone doing what needs to be done by me

- I eat chocolate chip cookies
- I often blame someone else or become angry with them

Examples of "because"

- I am afraid of what others might think, say or do
- I am afraid of looking foolish, being rejected, facing my fears
- I don't really like myself well enough to take care of my body
- I don't want to look at my real issues

When we get into our "becauses," we may find that what we thought we believed, or we *want* to believe is different from what we say we believe. It is at this point where we can begin to make progress toward Congruence.

In the example of the "because" being "I don't really like myself well enough to take care of my body," you may have excused poor health or conditioning in yourself by believing that you inherited an inferior genetic code or that you are too old to start exercising. After a while you adopt that as your professed belief. In fact, as you more carefully examine yourself, you find that you've just never felt you were worthy of good health. If you are unable to resolve these issues by yourself, seek competent professional help.

ଙ  ଙ  ଙ

We all have different beliefs and behaviors. And, since psychologists haven't figured everything out, I'm not going to make the attempt here. However, taking a close look at your beliefs and your actions is the first step in the practice of Congruence.

The next step in the practice of Congruence is to get a clear picture of how you are handling your priorities. Not long ago in a meeting, those of us in attendance were asked to speak for one minute on our priorities in life. Several of the people who spoke referred to family or faith or health being their top priority in life, but added, "… even though it may not look like it from the outside."

When it was my turn, I said that, if it didn't look like it was a priority in their life, then it really wasn't one, because we make time for our true priorities. There was a profound silence in the room for several moments as this truth sank in.

The next Congruence exercise will help you examine your priorities and how you are addressing them.

In my book, *The New Success,* is an exercise in which readers are asked to determine which six out of forty Life Qualities, such as achievement, security, health, or inner peace, are the most important to them. You may refer to that list if you have the book, or just use your own feelings and thoughts on the topic as you do this exercise.

## *Exercise 27:*
## *Setting Priorities*

In your notebook list the top five Life Qualities in your life.

List the top five priorities in your life.

Reconstruct the previous three days of your life. List what you did, hour by hour. You don't have to give minute-by-minute details, but it should be itemized enough so that you get a solid idea about how you are spending your time. Example:

Monday

6:30 woke up; 6:35-7:30 got ready for work 7:30-8:00 drove to work 8:00-5:00 worked; 5:00-5:30 drove home; 5:30-6:00 changed clothes, read mail, etc. 6:00-6:30 cooked dinner; 6:30-7:00 ate; 7:00-7:30 talked on the phone; 7:30-8:00 cleaned house; 8:00-10:00 watched TV; 10:00-10:30 got ready for bed; 10:30 went to bed.

You might include the activities on one of your free days, as your unstructured days often indicate more about how you spend your time. And, I hope leisure or pleasurable activities have an important role in your life.

Check back to your list of priorities. Highlight everything in your time log that contributes to one or more of those priorities. If you listed career as one of your priorities, then break down your work day into fifteen minute segments (I am *not* kidding) to see how you prioritize your day. I do this about every three months. The results often shock and embarrass me. It's so easy to become slack and let slide those things which are truly important. If I were to tell you your priorities by looking at your time reconstruction, would they match the five you have just listed? If not, examine either your professed priorities or your behaviors. One needs to change.

If more than seventy-five percent your time is spent on your priorities, then you are probably spending your time in congruence with what you say is important to you. Seventy-five percent may seem like an unrealistic figure, but, do you want to spend more than twenty-five percent of your waking hours doing that which is unimportant and even unpleasant to you?

If your time log reveals that you are spending an inordinate amount of time on trivial matters that do not contribute to your priorities, you need to examine both your time and your priorities. Be aware that your priorities may change and not notify you, so this is a good exercise to do every so often.

Our priorities also change over time to a particular Focus suited for each phase of our lives. In other words, young adults may be intensely Focused on finishing a college degree or getting that first job. At age twenty-one, owning a house and starting a family may not be a priority, even though that is a goal. If they have a family when they're still building their career, the time they spend with them may be minimized as they pour their energy into getting established. So, although family may be important as a Life Quality, it takes a back seat temporarily as a priority. When the people at the meeting were saying that their lives didn't reflect their priorities, they were really saying, "I'd like to have this as a priority, but right now I'm not choosing to."

It's important to understand the difference between Life Qualities and Priorities. A priority is what you make important by spending time, money, effort and concentration on. A Life Quality is something that is necessary for you to feel fulfilled.

You will not fulfill your destiny if your core beliefs, significant Life Qualities, priorities and behaviors are consistently out of line with each other. It will require too much energy to maintain equilibrium. Although ideally they will all match up, the occasional urgent situation may occur which causes you to move one to the back burner. You must then strive to get back in balance as quickly as possible.

Many of the beliefs we hold (and have learned) are in direct conflict with fulfilling our destiny. We must root them out and change those that are in conflict. Fred was a marketing expert working for a large corporation. His belief was that he needed to be employed by a big company in order to make the income he wanted. One of his most significant Life Qualities was honesty. He knew that the essence of his destiny had to do with communication. Although he drew a handsome salary, he often had no choice as to the clients with whom he worked. Some were unscrupulous and wanted him to produce less than honest marketing campaigns. Fred was in turmoil about the incongruity between his belief that he couldn't make this kind of income working on his own and his belief and need to produce honest campaigns. Through working with the Practices, he realized that his core belief about his employment was impeding his progress and he was able to change it. Today he works from his home office with clients of his own choosing, making more money than he was at the large agency. Through changing his belief, he was able to change his behavior and live more congruently.

If you say that you want to remember and fulfill your destiny, but you consistently make the decision to spend your meditation/quiet time doing something else, you are not behaving in a manner in Congruence with your statement. Either you do not believe that you can fulfill your destiny or your Intention to do so is impure. Either way, you are not being truthful with yourself or others. If, on the other hand, you sincerely seek your destiny and continue to chip away at it, even if it takes a long while, you will surely find it and you will begin living more and more congruently with your destiny.

The next exercises will help you get an idea of where you are in that process.

## *Exercise 28:*
## *Ten Minute Drill — Blocks*

Write your latest Destiny Statement on a clean sheet of paper in your notebook.

Under your Destiny Statement write for ten minutes on the following subject: "From what I know so far about my destiny, what am I doing/what do I believe that may get in the way of its fulfillment?"

## *Exercise 29:*
### *Into Action*

Review the log you kept about your activities. On a clean sheet of paper write down five activities that are in Congruence with your Destiny Statement.

Write five activities in which you will engage during the coming week that will put you more in Congruence with your Destiny Statement.

෯   ෯   ෯

As you get more and more insight into your destiny, you will want to bring your life more fully into alignment with it. When I first started my business, like most new business people, I needed work to keep the doors open. As a result, I took on many projects for which I was qualified, but which didn't really fulfill the Destiny Statement I had formulated for myself.

As a result, I found myself struggling more and more, wondering if I had made the right decision in leaving a well-paying job. As I pondered this, the answer came to me. Spirit said, "Do you want to make a living or do you want to make a difference?" My answer, of course, was that I wanted to make a difference and I wanted to live out my destiny. At that point I made the decision that I would no longer accept projects that did not contribute to my Destiny

Statement. In fact, I asked Spirit to keep them from even coming my way.

At first, it was a little scary, as much of my income had come from these other projects. In short order, however, things turned around and I found myself receiving projects that not only paid well but which were congruent with my definition of a Toolbringer.

It is now time in the journey of fulfilling your destiny and develop your Personal Manifesto. In its pure form, a manifesto is a public declaration of one's principles or intentions. The congruence and integrity with which you live your life is as important as your accomplishments. Most people carry in their minds a set of standards they more or less follow. Most of us are honest people, willing to serve the world and our fellow man to the best of our abilities. Yet, how much time have we really put into committing to paper a set of standards by which we intend to live?

The National Speakers Association, an organization of professional speakers, has a Code of Ethics which all members pledge to uphold. Yet, I have seen behavior from a few members I would certainly not classify as professional or ethical, even though those individuals did not violate the Code.

Doctors pledge to do no harm, yet, according to recent figures, more than 160,000 people die each year from prescription drugs. Lawyers, accountants and all other professionals have legal and moral standards to which they, technically, must adhere, yet a few push so far to the edge of their standards that we wonder if the criteria for ethical behavior has meaning any more.

It is the responsibility of each of us consciously to determine the basis for expression of this life. For each of us it is a little different. Rather than being a statement of specific goals, a Manifesto is a map of your character. It describes how you will face the day to day as well as the difficult events of your life.

In essence, a Manifesto can make life easier. It helps us to remove moral dilemmas from our lives as we commit to a certain way of living.

## *Exercise 30:*
## *Building Your Manifesto*

Here is a step-by-step process for building your Personal Manifesto. You have already done part of the work.

1. Review the notes you have written so far in your Destiny work. In your Destiny Notebook write key words from your Intention statements that reflect values important to you, such as honesty, integrity, honor, peace, or joy. Add any other words or phrases that come to mind. Don't edit your thoughts at this point. Just write.

2. Fashion these words and phrases into a personal Manifesto of not more than one page.

3. Post your Manifesto where you will see it often. Read it every day and make changes

as appropriate. Strive to live within its parameters.

I must, each day, make conscious decisions about my
priorities. Like almost everyone, I have infinite choices.
Some of the decisions I've made have been difficult. Some
times, I'd rather be lazy and just play computer games all
day. But, holding the Intention of taking steps each day to
fulfill my destiny, I always do *something* in that direction.
Each day I strive to live a little more congruently with that
which is my Destiny.

# Chapter 11

# *World Service*

World Service is the practice that reflects the application of all the other practices. At the blueprint level your destiny was designed so you could contribute your talents and skills to the world. At birth, the strands of your DNA were intricately woven into the perfect configuration for you to step out and take your place in service to our world.

You were born at precisely the right time to the perfect parents for your destiny, and you have experienced exactly what you needed to bring you to this point. You are reading this book at exactly the right time for you to trigger the events needed to fulfill your destiny.

What is World Service when we talk about it in the context of the Twelve Practices? It is that which you do with the gifts and talents you've been given. It is how you apply the insights you receive. It concerns itself with what you are giving.

To carry out your World Service, you do not need to dress in sack cloth and become a homeless wanderer. That's generally neither practical nor required. However, you will want to examine what you do with your life and your time and give some thought to how it serves the world. World Service concerns itself not only with your vocation, but with your avocations as well.

Although you may be in a vocation that aligns precisely with what you know about your destiny, as you proceed through level after level of Initiation, you may find yourself in what seems to be a constant examination of your appropriate World Service. What is perfectly suited to you now may be a stepping stone to the next level of World Service. Never assume that you have "arrived" at World Service any more than you ever arrive at completion of the other Twelve Practices. It is an on-going process.

As I mentioned previously, I was once shown my destiny and its outpicturing in this life. In that vision, I saw myself speaking before crowds of people. On a table beside me lay a stack of books, each with a different title, but with the same author — me. At the time I was employed by a large corporation. Fortunately, I enjoyed my job and knew it was leading me forward, although I couldn't have guessed the direction it was taking.

I was both fascinated and frightened by this vision. I had always wanted to write a book, but never had in mind to do more than one. I had written several articles and edited some corporate newsletters. I had also written numerous training programs both for the corporation and for our church lay ministry program. I was guided to take an advanced writing class to further my skill. In other words, I had worked hard to sharpen my skills.

Not long thereafter, I taught a series of classes at my company on career development. In that class, participants were asked to take a look at their jobs and several job steps in the future. They were then asked to describe some fantasy job they had dreamed about, such as concert musician, professional baseball player, or anything that struck their fancy. During the exercise, they were asked to numerically rank all the jobs, based on various factors such as values and lifestyle. Almost all the participants gave the highest scores to their current jobs or the job just above them. The purpose of the exercise was to demonstrate that most of them either were currently in positions that suited them or were ready for the next step.

As the teacher, I had to demonstrate how to do this, so I used my vision as my fantasy job. Over the months I found that the scores for my fantasy job grew closer and closer to the scores for my current job. Then the scores surpassed them until, finally, the score for the fantasy job, my vision, got so high that I had to dream up a new fantasy just to make the proper demonstration for the class.

At the time that my scores in the class were growing, my satisfaction with my job (which had by then changed) and the ethics surrounding that situation were plummeting. I realized that, not only could I not remain in a position that required that much compromise, but that I was being called to fulfill my destiny.

My years with the corporation had been absolutely appropriate for me. The company spent thousands of dollars educating me (for which they received good measure from me) and preparing me to fulfill my destiny. When the experience was through, I was placed in a position that made it almost impossible to stay. I had received some "cosmic" hints earlier that it was time to leave, but, as I always maintain, if we don't take the hint, God gives us His loving boot on our behinds.

The expression of my World Service has evolved since I left my "real" job and became independent of that world, but always I have been reaching toward fulfilling my destiny as a Toolbringer. When I develop new material for my corporate or spiritual engagements or for articles, I always ask, "Will this give the audience or readers a new tool to make their lives better? Will it call them to a higher expression of themselves?" If the answer is no, I redo the material.

Where are you in your expression of World Service? You may feel that you are not in a very good job or that your life is not a reflection of your destiny. The best place to start is where you are.

## *Exercise 31:*
### *World Service on the Job*

In this exercise you are going to bring your destiny to the job, no matter what that job is. Use the following sequence tomorrow before you leave for work.

When you first wake up, give thanks for having made it through the night. Then give thanks for your current state. If you have a job, give thanks for it, even if you dread going there. If you are looking for work, give thanks for Divine

Order working for you in that direction. If you work in the home, give thanks for the circumstances that allow it.

Arise and go to a quiet place with a paper and pen. If you have to get up early, so be it. Develop the Discipline to do so. Become still and decide what your Intention for the day is. Write that down. I use my daily planner for this exercise so I look at it all day as a reminder. Then, ask for guidance about your highest World Service for the day. The basic difference between Intention and World Service is that Intention most often refers to an attitude or inner approach, as described in Chapter Three. World Service is usually more outwardly Focused. Write down the first thing that comes to mind. It may or may not make sense.

One day I received "peace" as my guidance both for World Service and for Intention. I wrote it in my planner, even though at the time I was puzzled by it. The first person to come crashing through my office door that morning was a very angry manager from another department. If I had not committed to peace as my World Service for the day, I might have responded differently and contributed to chaos instead. Adding my bit to a peaceful attitude that day was the highest service I could have rendered my world. By my holding to my Intention, we came to a swift resolution with neither of us needing to compromise our principles or our sanity.

Other days I have been guided toward more mundane forms of World Service, such as cleaning my house or writing an article. Other times I feel led to step out of my comfort zone more than usual and take steps that are uncomfortable. These I attempt to do with as little whining as possible.

Meditate for a few minutes about your Intention and your highest World Service for the day. Jot down any insights you may have, then go about your business. As often as possible during the day, apply both your Intention and your World Service to the situation at hand.

You will find that, although things around you may not change appreciably, you will begin to transform. That which was formerly borderline, but acceptable, may not be so any longer.

Howard was a pharmaceutical representative. He was one of the top salesmen in his district and had won many awards from his company. His destiny statement crystallized into "Fixer." He began to get glimpses of himself helping people to repair their damaged bodies at a cellular level. Each day as he wrote his Intention and his World Service statements, he felt that he was living incongruently with his destiny. Although he was in a health-related field, he felt himself drawn more and more to natural healing methods rather than the drug industry. After months of planning and meditating, he left his lucrative position to attend a naturopathic college. He now has a thriving business which he feels is in concert with why he is here.

Jane was a financial planner at a small, but successful business. As she examined her destiny, she came up with the phrase, "keep them safe." At first she didn't want to look at her destiny because she thought she might have to give up the career she loved in order to follow something else. However, she finally realized how much the world needed deeply committed, honest individuals in positions that helped people with their economic decisions. She saw that she was in a perfect place to render World Service. As she dedicated herself increasingly to fulfilling her destiny, her clientele transitioned into people of a high spiritual nature who were completely compatible with her. Her part of the business has continued to grow and prosper. She will now work only with people who share her values and outlook.

You may be concerned that your World Service may not be fully expressed in your vocation. I know of several people who are in positions seemingly "beneath" them who use that simply as a means to pay the rent while they concentrate on something else. Others hold jobs that seem incongruent with their Destiny Statements. While in these positions, they bring a light and attitude to the workplace that uplifts everyone around them. This, too, is World Service.

Joel works as a waiter at a good restaurant. With the tips he receives, he makes a good income, even though the work is not intellectually challenging. He is the most popular waiter at the restaurant. Because of his ability to Focus on the diners and make them feel welcome, comfortable and appreciated, several patrons ask to be seated in his section, acknowledging his attention by leaving him generous tips. His real passion is as an unpaid volunteer, working with troubled youth, giving them hope and courage to grow up to fulfill their destinies. He said that the work with the children takes a lot of energy and working at the restaurant gives him a good break from the tension that often accompanies his volunteer work. At this point, he wouldn't change anything. And, the congruity with which he leads all facets of his life brings to him a good means of supporting himself.

This is what I mean when I say that your primary World Service may not appear to be totally in sync with your vocation. The following exercise may help you to understand more about how you can begin to apply World Service right where you are. If for some reason you need to change to a different line of work, it will help you to grow in that direction.

## *Exercise 32:*
## *Expressing World Service*

On a clean sheet in your Destiny Journal complete the following statements:

- My destiny statement, as I know it to date is:
- My current vocation is:
- This contributes to my World Service in the following ways:
- I can bring greater service to this vocation by:
- I can express service outside my vocation by:

If you are in a place where you are expressing your true World Service, you will experience joy in its accomplishment. You will, for the most part, look forward to being involved in it. Your World Service may be demonstrated in activities for which you are paid in money or you may be drawn to activities for which your reward is inner satisfaction. One may feed into the other.

During your day, you can contribute to your World Service in wonderful ways. As often as you remember, ask, "What can I do right now as a part of my World Service?" Listen for a response, using the practice of Access. At first, you may not notice a response. If that is the case, simply continue with the task in which you were involved. Soon, however, if you continue to ask, you will receive answers. These answers may not always come from within. Sometimes, at the very moment you ask, another person may provide the answer. Or, you may read a sentence that "knocks you over." At other times, you will feel led to make a phone call. Sometimes you will know that you are doing exactly the right activity for your World Service at that moment.

The guidance you receive will usually not be dramatic. It almost always involves some small or routine task that takes you one step further on your path.

Many years ago I was scheduled to take a typing test to be hired into a company. I visited the library to check out a typing book for practice. As I headed for the check out desk, I casually asked God if that was all. The reply was so loud I looked around to see if anyone else heard it. "Get a shorthand dictation record," it bellowed. Having taken shorthand in college to compensate for my too-slow note taking, I complied. For three days I practiced some typing and a lot of shorthand, not even knowing why.

When I arrived at the test, the manager asked our large group of applicants, "Does anyone here know shorthand in addition to typing?" I was the only one who raised her hand. The manager took me into a special room for a separate test.

As a result, I got a much better job than I anticipated at a wonderful salary. In fact, following that advice led not only to a successful career at that company, but the first day on the job, I met the man who would become my husband. That certainly convinced me about the practicality of listening for advice about what to do next!

While I was still employed by the corporation, I was the training director for the lay ministry program at my church. I spent countless hours developing programs that would help the candidates uncover their own spirituality and areas of service right for them. I also developed sessions that expanded their knowledge base. Although I didn't receive any money for this work, it was invaluable in preparing me for the work I do now. Many people who went through that program continued on to find extraordinary growth in their lives and careers.

Everything you have experienced, no matter what, contributes to your ability to now express perfect World Service. Let go of regrets and cease to agonize over choices that you feel were in error. Each new moment is an opportunity to begin again. You have a moment to moment choice to start living in the flow of your Destiny. Nothing changes the past, however, you can decide if your future will fulfill your Destiny.

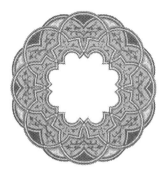

*Chapter 12*

# *Initiation*

Throughout the ages, man has participated in many forms of Initiation, marking the passages of life, inductions into societies, or crossing the thresholds into new levels of consciousness. Some of the Initiation ceremonies in which I have taken part, such as being confirmed in my church, have held great significance for me. I attended classes for months in preparation and was well aware that it marked my passage into adulthood as far as the church was concerned. It was a time of great spiritual growth for me as well. Other Initiations have seemed a little silly to me. (I won't enumerate those, as those same Initiation ceremonies may have had great meaning for some of you.)

Initiation at its basic level is a series of steps that we must experience each time we shed outgrown modes of being and adapt new patterns and beliefs. We experience many forms of Initiation in life, often without understanding or acknowledging them.

Sometimes you experience a moving Initiation at a very deep level. Other times you may feel angry or depressed without knowing why, even when things are going well.

It may be that during these unsettling times, you are undergoing an Initiation, when everything that is unlike the new you is falling away. You are saying good-bye to a part of you that is familiar and comfortable. Even though this old part no longer serves you, the sense of separation can cause you a literal sense of mourning, like when you lose a very good friend.

When, Delores began using the Visualization exercise in Chapter Four, she encountered several difficulties. She felt that everything in her life was falling apart, and she was ready to just give up all her progress. In fact, this is the time when most people give up on their dreams. In essence, she was shedding the old Delores so that she could take on a new, brighter, more successful self.

Anytime we shed an old skin, it's bound to be painful. I convinced her to continue with the work and within a few weeks, her life had transformed beyond all belief. But, she needed the purifying fire of initiation to emerge.

In ancient times, candidates for priesthood often attended what were called mystery schools, much like priests today attend seminary. These candidates, called adepts, were required to pass ever more difficult initiatory levels before finally being accepted into the inner circles of the mystery schools or priesthoods. In many cases, at the top level of Initiations, these practices were so dangerous that many initiates lost their lives in the attempt. They were often required to figure out complex problems or Focus on certain principles in order to pass through the various barriers, often illusory, that were placed in their way. If they failed, it was usually because they succumbed to the illusions that were placed before them instead of keeping their minds Focused on the goal, or their destination. Before they were allowed to participate in an Initiation process they were required to complete rigorous study and strenuous training. Their mentors did everything possible to prepare them for each level of Initiation. In the same way, even though we may not recognize it, we are being prepared for each Initiation we undergo. If we are aware of the process, we will pass through each Initiation in ways that will be less unsettling and more satisfying than if we succumb to the illusions created by ignorance or loss of Focus.

As you attend this mystery school called Life on Earth, and pass each Initiation, you may feel that you are on the brink of losing everything. But, as of old, if you see beyond the illusion, you will find the truth.

You have taken a lifetime (and many believe several lifetimes) to accumulate the debris of misconceptions. Layer upon layer has been carefully applied and glued into your psyche. As you peel away each stratum of illusion, you will experience some sort of Initiation. As far as I can tell, you will never arrive at the point where there are no more Initiations. This process is lifelong, ongoing and exciting. You can learn to recognize this process and, although you will still go through the experience, understanding the cause of your discomfort can go a long way towards hastening its end.

I can tell you about my own experience with Initiation and from that you can look at yours and begin to discern a pattern.

In my own process I have undergone two types of Initiations. The first I have already described to you, which is, the outer ceremonial kind. This is sometimes followed by the second sort of Initiation — the inner Initiation. Inner Initiation is the one that marks the real growth and generally precipitates some sort of lasting change in life. The actual inner Initiation may be consciously sought or it may just sort of creep up on you and surprise you.

My first inner Initiation is a moving and beautiful memory that I cherish. It came to me, unbidden, during meditation. I suddenly found myself in another place and time, with a dark-haired man acting as my teacher. At other times I have found myself (in consciousness) in Egypt, in a temple, in a hidden cave on a hillside, and simply in the same room in which I am meditating. Each time a meaningful ceremony was conducted in which I have been shown symbols or given messages that let me know that I have grown to a new level of understanding and wisdom. I emerge from these meditations knowing that something important has just happened.

These wonderful experiences almost always follow a time of emotional difficulty, when I have shed the skin of some old part of me. Many traditions refer to this as The Dark Night of the Soul. Virtually everyone I know who is awakening to his destiny has struggled through these difficulties, so I have learned to welcome them. (Although, I'm not sure if my friends and family welcome them as do I.

After all, they have to put up with me while I'm going through them!)

The good news is that the skin slips off more easily now, sometimes in a matter of hours rather than weeks or months. I've even learned recognize the symptoms. In my case, I become angry and begin to remember all sorts of injustices that have been done to me over the years. It took me a while to realize that they are mostly old patterns being released. In other words, they are everything that is unlike the emerging me. The old ways of thinking can't get out unless they go through me. So, I wave them good-bye.

The next step is futility. (Remember, these are *my* steps. Yours may be different.) One of my friends and I refer to this as the "My Life Has No Meaning" phase. We now actually find this stage very funny. (By the way, you will begin to find more and more humor as you grow and notice the pettiness in so many of our imagined hurts and angers.)

After that comes the Initiation, the breakthrough. It is that dawn into which we step with an expanded vision and a new awareness. The trick is to understand what is happening to us and to keep going during each step of Initiation. The good news is that, unlike the old mystery schools, we get more chances at Initiation if we back away.

While undergoing the Initiation process, you may notice yourself going through four distinct phases. They may happen very rapidly or over a period of several months. (At the end of this chapter is a ritual you may wish to perform to trigger your next Initiation.) A ceremony may heighten or accelerate the process, but, ultimately, it is you who completes the Initiation from within.

The first phase of Initiation — ***Disconnection*** — is a sense of restlessness, a vague feeling that the current status is about to, or needs to, change. In this case, I am referring to inner status, even though an outward event, such as an argument, may provoke this inner feeling. You may find yourself questioning a lifelong belief or relationship or you may feel as though you've outgrown your present position.

Remember that it doesn't have to be an "earth-shaking" feeling. In fact, it is often more subtle, like a vague restlessness. You will grow to recognize this sense of disconnection as you move through several Initiations. At first it can be quite unsettling if you don't know what's happening. What many people call a "midlife crisis" is actually the beginning of an Initiation. Properly recognized, it can lead to deeper relationships and more satisfying World Service. Unfortunately, too many people fail to recognize the signs and leave behind them shattered families and broken careers. Being able to recognize the signs of an Initiation when they happen can be an important step toward a healthy growth.

"I don't get it," complained Joanne. "I have everything I ever wanted, and, yet, for some reason, I feel I need something else."

I explained to her that this was the beginning of an initiatory process for her and a natural part of growth. It must be like the hermit crab deciding to find a bigger shell, even though the one she is living in may seem adequate. When is the time right to move to a larger shell? She just knows. Through our conversations, Joanne prepared herself for the second phase — ***Opening.***

In my practice I use a product called Destiny Cards to help people unfold. Each of the ninety cards contains a question beginning with "What if..." By selecting a card and writing a Ten-Minute Drill to answer the question, people generally gain new levels of understanding and awareness. Joanne began exploring the step of Opening by drawing a different card each morning and writing a Ten-Minute Drill. Her first card was, "What if I used all my gifts and talents to their full potential?" This helped her to open herself to the revelations that highlight the Initiation process. For a week she drew a new card each day, writing her drill then carrying the card with her throughout the day and referring to it to gain further insights. On the eighth day she read the card that led her to the third step in the Initiation process — ***Revelation.*** Her card that day said, "What if I fearlessly followed my heart?"

The Revelation step is often sudden and startling. In dramatic situations there is a deep illumination. In Joanne's case, she realized that she was carrying around an old fear which was holding her back from expressing herself through painting. As a child, she had been severely punished for drawing when she was supposed to have been practicing her arithmetic, so she had a vague fear of punishment whenever she picked up her art materials. She was able to "exorcise" that demon and move on to the final step — ***Activation.***

Joanne began taking art classes and found she had a latent talent for calligraphy. She now joyfully letters pictures, cards, and other beautiful items that produce a nice income and provide beauty and pleasure to those who receive them. During this process, she also discovered that a part of her destiny included increasing beauty in the world. Her calligraphy certainly contributes to that destiny, as well as earning a nice living.

Activation is the phase that many overlook in the initiatory process. We must take forth the knowledge we gain in the initiatory process and apply it to that which we know of our destiny.

Some people find it helpful to perform an outer ritual to help them precipitate an inner Initiation experience. About a year ago I was feeling a little "spiritual sluggishness." I had a feeling that I was close to another Initiation, but couldn't seem to get myself Focused enough to bring it about. I was moved to attend an Initiation ceremony given by Jo Dunning, an extraordinary teacher. I remember very little about the actual outer ritual. About two minutes into it, I was "transported" to a mountain, led along the ledge of a cliff and taken deep into a cave where a ceremony, completely unrelated to the one taking place in the outer, was performed. At this point I am not free to give you the details of the inner Initiation, but, attending the outer rite helped me to experience the inner growth. As you experience your Initiations, you, too, may find that you are asked not to reveal the details. This is not unusual.

In one case, two colleagues and I performed an Initiation ritual which most of the participants found to be quite powerful. It was a combination of a laying on of hands and a spiritual baptism. Several experienced breakthroughs during the ritual or shortly after. However, one delightful gentleman said in good humor when it was over, "Well, that was a nice piece of fluff," and went off to bed.

Later I learned he was up all night being ill. Perhaps his body was ready to get rid of that which no longer suited it and move on to a healthier expression.

જી  જી  જી

During a deep Initiation you may find yourself feeling stripped bare emotionally. It can be quite unsettling. However, if you understand what is going on, even though you may still feel despair, you will be able to come through it at a much higher level and with less drama. Believe me, it will be easier on you and on everyone around you.

The Initiation ritual in this book is an outward act which helps to put you in the proper frame of mind for true Initiation. This tradition is familiar to many Christians in rituals such as Communion or Baptism.

Marriage is an Initiation ritual as old as civilization, the purpose of which is to initiate not only the bride and groom, but all of their society into their new status and new relationship.

I use the metaphor of Initiation to describe these stages of growth because they share common characteristics with ancient and modern Initiations.

One similarity is the belief that we are somehow being tested or put through a trial. This is part of the purification process in growth. And, with each stage of Initiation, we fear moving forward. Eventually we leave behind a part of us that no longer fits, and we gain new understanding, but at the same time, we take on new responsibilities. We may not be sure we are capable of handling this new role, so we may hesitate.

It may be at this very threshold between the old self and the new role that we turn back, never realizing our destiny or stepping into the magnificence in which we were created. Sometimes, instead, we abdicate fate and simply give up. However, as long as we are willing to knock on the door, sincerely, one more time, we are given the opportunity to meet the destiny that is rising up before us. It is never too late.

Another element of Initiation, both ancient and modern, is sacrifice. In ancient times, it was common to sacrifice an animal or person as part of an Initiation ritual. Fortunately, you no longer need to find a chicken to roast on an altar. Today the concept of sacrifice as part of Initiation is letting go of what no longer suits you. You may have to sacrifice a cherished belief, an old grudge, a fear that holds you back or a toxic relationship. Most times, the thing you sacrifice is returned to you in a different and higher form.

It is this sacrifice, this giving up of something cherished, that leads to what the ancients called The Dark Night Of The Soul. Jesus experienced it in the Garden of Gesthemene when he was preparing for his unpleasant sacrifice which would result in his greater glory. We often identify with this as we are going through the pre-Initiation struggles. We can feel alone and frightened, even pleading with God to take the cup (the pain of sacrifice) away. If we stay the course, however, the dawn of the next phase of our existence will come. It is as if the stone has been rolled away and the doorway opened.

The doorways in our lives symbolize those times when we gain awareness and, thus, Initiation into another level of living. It is by plunging into the darkness of the other side of these doorways that our lives are enriched, even if the barriers seem insurmountable and the way impassable.

When the darkness is absolute and we cannot see even a few inches ahead, the trial we are passing through is exactly the challenge we need to open up the next phase. If you are diligently practicing in the other eleven areas, you may be noticing that you are gaining a greater awareness of the cycles you are going through.

This awareness does not necessarily remove the obstacles; however knowing they are merely markers along your journey helps you to remain more peaceful and less attached to the outcome.

You may find your confidence in facing these obstacles increasing as you step securely forward, knowing that, as you Access the information you need, take the action that needs to be taken by you, and Forgive that which needs to be Forgiven, the light in the situation grows brighter and your steps become lighter. You may, in fact, look back upon the situation and wonder what the fuss was about. At that point, your dawn will have arrived.

Sometimes the light may well emerge after we have given up the physical body. Last year a dear friend passed away. He was well into his eighties and had lived a rich, full life. His wife had gone on about five years earlier and he had not really been the same since. The night he died, I was sending him love and doing what I could at a soul level to ease his passing. I suddenly saw him before me, but he wasn't lying in his bed. He was jogging into a meadow. Waiting there for him was his wife with her arms open. Young and beautiful again, they danced and hugged and rejoiced for several minutes before walking off, arm in arm. I knew I had seen him emerging from his dark night, passing through his Initiation, and emerging into a new form. Sad at his passing, I also exulted in his joy.

In ancient times, and in many modern Initiation rites, candidates were required to purify their bodies, often by fasting and/or ritual bathing, as a symbol that even their bodies were ready for the next step.

When I sense that an Initiation is immanent, I will take more notice of what I eat. Even though I eat a generally healthy diet, I eliminate animal products and drink much more water than usual. This serves to heighten the clarity of my thought, not to mention the good it does my body. At the same time, I begin to purify my mind by taking more time in meditation and "bathing" myself in even more positive literature and music than normal. As I am bathing, I pretend that I am preparing myself for Initiation. In this way I become more and more receptive to the event that will transpire. I wish I could give you a formula for when to do this. In my case, I just somehow sense it is time. If you pay attention, you will probably arrive at the knowledge on your own. (That's one of the annoyances with mysticism. You need to figure some of this out by yourself.)

Years ago a friend asked me how I knew it was time to leave my corporate job and go out on my own. Sensing she was wrestling with the same decision, I said, "You'll just know." She gave me a puzzled look, but nodded. About four months later, she came up to me and said, "Guess what?" I answered, "You know?" She said, "I know." Within a few weeks she had left her job to start her own business.

When you are ready to perform the following ritual, I recommend you set a date with yourself a week in advance. This will give you time to purify yourself and to make yourself ready for the experience. It may well be that you will receive an Initiation during the preparatory period and, of course, it will be just as meaningful, so accept it if it comes early.

You may do as I do to prepare or you may have other ideas, such as preparing an area in your house to perform the ritual. You may wish to set up an altar upon which you place some of your sacred objects. You may listen to music that feeds your spirit.

You may even wish to perform a daily ritual of some sort as a preparation, such as lighting a candle on your altar or saying certain prayers. People in the Catholic church sometimes hold a nine-day vigil called Novena in which they pray and fast for nine days, knowing that their prayers will be answered. Other people literally lock themselves in a room to fast and pray for three or four days in preparation. Still others feel no need to do anything in the outer. They simply ask for Initiation. Try more than one approach to preparing for Initiation to discover what is most suitable for you. Now that you have experienced the practice of Access, you may use that skill to ask what your procedure should be.

It really doesn't matter when you perform your ritual. I will be referring to the time as night or evening, as that is

the time most people prefer. What matters is the significance with which you view it. Consider some of the
following activities that may make the ceremony richer for
you.

When you schedule your initiation rite, try to do so on
an evening before a day when you have nothing scheduled.
That will give you the next day to consider what transpired
and to remain in a contemplative state. Eat as lightly as
possible in the hours before you begin. If possible, ingest
nothing but pure water. (Please follow your health practi-
tioner's counsel if you have a medical condition.) Watch no
television nor read newspapers. Listen to beautiful, soothing
music. Shower or bathe just before the ritual as a symbolic
cleansing. Many religions emphasize bathing prior to going
into the temple. Some  initiates retire for the night then get
up at midnight for the ceremony, staying up in meditation
the rest of the night and greeting the dawn with thanksgiving.

Approach the Initiation ritual without any preconceived ideas about what might happen. In fact, you may
prepare carefully for days and, at the end, feel that nothing
has happened. In fact, any time you perform a ritual such as
this with an Intention of growth, something happens. It may
be on an inner level that will not manifest on the outside for
sometime. A change may happen gradually over a period of
several weeks. After one of the first intentional ceremonies
I performed, I enjoyed the experience, but didn't sense any
change. However, about two days later I found myself
becoming very angry about small, almost insignificant
events that had happened long ago. I realized that my body

was cleansing itself of old hurts that were no longer appropriate to my new level of being. I was able to release these events from my life and move on. On another occasion, I was directed to a better way of eating that resulted in a higher energy level and better health.

## *Exercise 33:*
## *Initiation Ritual*

Prepare the room where you will perform your ceremony. Have a large glass or bottle of pure water available to drink as you please during the ritual. Photocopy the ceremony or bring this book with you. If it is more convenient, you may wish to record the ceremony and listen to it or order the tape from the author.

Place a straight-back chair, such as a dining room chair, in the room. If you have an altar, put the chair facing it. If possible, conduct the initiation by candlelight, taking standard safety precautions. Have enough light near your chair so you are able to read the ceremony.

Stand in front of your chair. Read the following aloud:

*"I now ask for protection and blessings on what is about to occur and I allow only that which is from God to enter into this space. I have prepared and purified myself and aspire to grow and to learn. I ask that I be initiated into the next level of my growth. I stand ready to receive that which is for my highest good."*

Breathe deeply and slowly for about a minute, then be seated. Keep your back straight and your feet flat on the floor. Read the following aloud:

*"I now ask that I be cleansed further and prepared for entry into the upper chamber.*

[Picture a light coming up through the center of the earth and entering the soles of your feet. See this light traveling up your legs, cleansing any impurities. Watch it slowly move through your entire body, pausing wherever there is a blockage, cleansing and healing that area. Feel the light moving out through the top of your head, taking all impurities with it. You may notice the light turning a different color as it collects your internal "pollution." When the light exits your body, picture the impurities being completely consumed by a violet light, gone forever from your being. After you have experienced this, sit quietly for ten minutes, contemplating what might have just been cleansed from you.]

When you have finished, read the following aloud:

*"I completely surrender to the work of God within me, quickening all the cells of my body and leading me higher. I ask for a word or symbol to guide me during the next phase of my growth. I ask that this word or symbol be revealed to me in such a manner that I cannot possibly mistake it."*

Again become still until you are aware of a word or symbol forming before you. You may hear it, sense it or see it. Or, after several minutes you may feel guided to continue with the rest of the ceremony, knowing your symbol will be revealed to you shortly. Many people stumble upon their symbols quite by non-accident within a few days of completing the ritual, so don't worry if nothing is revealed to you at this moment. This is so personal that I cannot give you further guidance about it. Just remain open to the experience.

When you feel a sense of completion with this section, read the following aloud:

> *"I now ask to receive guidance about the next step on my journey. I give thanks in advance for this knowledge and hold the Intention to carry through with it."*

Again sit in the silence, open to any guidance you receive. Remain receptive for several minutes, again knowing that if you do not experience any specific guidance, it will show up soon. We each have our own perfect timing.

When you have finished with this section, read the following aloud:

> *"I give thanks for my perfect experience and go forward expressing my higher self in all situation. I live in integrity and peace, fulfilling my Destiny and walking the path of divine order. All is well and it is so."*

If you wish to continue sitting in the silence, feel free to do so. Otherwise, extinguish your candle and turn on a light. Record your experience in your notebook.

During the next several days, remain open for signs that indicate you have grown to a new level. Begin each day with thanksgiving and end it with forgiveness.

છ   છ   છ

In the dictionary, the word "initiate" can mean either a novice, someone just beginning a journey or a formal initiation, or it can mean someone who has been initiated into a higher order. In our journey, no matter how many initiations we undergo, we are always initiates. As soon as we are initiated into a level higher than before, we begin the journey again, climbing higher, seeking the full expression of our destinies.

I place Initiation last in the Practices — not because of its level of importance. All of the practices are equally important. It is here because it needs the foundation of all the other practices to support it. You must learn to Access the voice of Spirit, whispering to you about your destiny. You need to have developed the ability to Articulate not only your destiny statement but that which you want and need in life. If you cannot Visualize to some extent at least some part of your destiny, you will not be able to clearly Project it. If you are still involved in creating great dramas or in holding grudges against anyone, you cannot develop the Congruence needed to fulfill that which is outlined in your blueprint. If you have not mastered the Discipline to develop at a beginning level the first ten Practices, you will not be prepared for your Initiations. And, if you have not built a solid foundation of the first ten Practices, your ability to fully manifest your perfect World Service will be withheld from you.

The Twelve Practices are all inter-connected. The web is spun. It is now your job to secure it from the wind by continuing to strengthen it. As the web you fashion becomes stronger, it will connect with those constructed by others. As we all begin to understand more and more about our combined destinies and how the blueprints designed for each of us are part of a grand pattern, together we will build a world in which remembering our destinies will be as natural as breathing.

# *Putting It All Together*

Throughout this book I have given you exercises and suggestions to help you not only remember the Destiny for which you were designed, but to help you create a life that is generally more satisfying. You have a lot of pieces, but may be wondering how to put them together and arrange the time for them in your busy schedule and hectic life.

In this chapter I'll show you some ways to approach this process so you are not overwhelmed but can make consistent progress.

First of all, you will need to Discipline yourself enough to set aside some time. You may need to look at all your activities and decide which ones can go. It was easy for me. I cut back on my housework. You can give up one television program a day. You can also get up fifteen minutes earlier. What about your lunch period? Find a way to spend it alone with your Destiny work. You can notify your family that in the evening, you will be in prayer and/or meditation for a half-hour and are not to be disturbed. If you hold an

Intention to put aside the time each day and don't allow outside influences to sway you, you will find a way. I found time when I was a single parent, working fifty to sixty hours a week and training for a marathon. If I can do it, you can do it.

Many students set aside fifteen minutes in the morning and fifteen minutes just prior to retiring as a sort of frame for the day. Even if you choose not to do that, take one minute when you first wake up to give thanks for being brought to the beginning of a new day. Realize that the day is new and so is your life. In your mind preview the day, seeing each event unfold for the good of all. Mentally set an Intention for the day. Write down that Intention as soon as you get a chance.

ȣ    ȣ    ȣ

If you want to follow the process as it is laid out in the book, follow the outline I give you for completing one round in forty days, or you can lay out your own schedule. I suggest you somehow track your progress in your Destiny notebook, as it helps you to stay on course.

Here is my suggestion for a Forty-Day Process that will take you through all the exercises and meditations in the book. This may or may not bring you to a total revelation as to your Destiny nor will following this process for a mere forty days put your life in order. However, if you are diligent and sincere, you will see changes.

## *Exercise 34:*
## *The Forty Day Destiny Process*

Read the entire book without stopping to do the exercises. Begin each day as outlined above. Write your Intention for the day.

*Day 1:*    Assemble your Destiny Notebook. Use a three-ring binder so you can insert pages. You may order a Destiny Notebook that contains all the materials you need to complete the process, by writing to the address in the back of the book. Put in plenty of lined notebook paper. Use your notebook both as a place to record your experiences and as a daily journal to track your progress. In each case, when I instruct you to practice an exercise or to complete a mediation, write your experiences in your Notebook. I won't tell you to do this each time. Practice Exercise 1.

*Day 2:*    Complete Meditation 1. Practice Exercise 2.

*Day 3:*    Complete Meditation 1, adding to the notes you took yesterday.

*Day 4:*    Complete Meditation 1, adding to your notes. Practice Exercise 3.

*Day 5:*    Practice Exercise 3. Complete Meditation 2.

*Day 6:*    Complete Meditation 2. Begin to formulate your Preliminary Destiny Statement.

*Day 7:*  Complete Meditation 2. Continue to formulate your Preliminary Destiny Statement.

*Day 8:*  Complete Meditation 2. Practice Exercise 4.

*Day 9:*  Write your Preliminary Destiny Statement at the top of the page of your Destiny Notebook each time you start a new page. Refine it as you wish as you go along.

*Day 10:*  Practice Exercise 5. Think about what you've learned to date.

*Day 11:*  Practice Exercise 6. If you haven't been doing so, write a Daily Intention each day for the remainder of the forty days.

*Day 12:*  Practice Exercise 7.

*Day 13:*  Practice Exercise 8.

*Day 14:*  Complete Meditation 3.

*Day 15:*  Complete Meditation 3 again.

*Day 16:*  Practice Exercise 9.

*Day 17:*  Practice Exercises 9 and 10. (Continue to practice Exercise 9 each day until you become proficient at it.) You may find that you are not able to complete your Six-Month Vision Statement in one sitting. Do as much as you can today.

*Day 18:*  Continue to refine your Six-Month Vision Statement. Practice the rest of Exercise 10.

*Day 19:*  Read your Six-Month Vision Statement as instructed in Exercise 10. Continue this as a daily practice until you feel a sense of completion. Continue Practicing Exercise 9.

***Day 20:***   Practice Exercise 11. Continue to set your Daily Intention and to read your Six-Month Vision Statement.

***Day 21:***   Make at least ten copies of the outline of the figure on Page 80. Practice Exercise 12 with as many of the alternatives as possible. Practice this exercise as often as you have a chance, not only during the forty days, but from now on.

***Day 22:***   Practice Exercise 13. Begin to implement steps to diffuse your own Victiming.

***Day 23:***   Practice Exercise 14. Practice this exercise whenever you desire something.

***Day 24:***   Practice Exercise 15.

***Day 25:***   Practice Exercise 16.

***Day 26:***   Practice Exercise 16.

***Day 27:***   Practice Exercises 17 and 18.

***Day 28:***   Practice Exercise 19. Continue daily practice until you can focus totally on your breath for ten minutes.

***Day 29:***   Practice Exercises 20 and 21.

***Day 30:***   Make several copies of the Scapegoat on page 127. Practice Exercise 22. (Tip: Keep a few blank copies with you for those frustrating moments of the day. It's a great way to work off stress!)

***Day 31:***   Practice Exercise 23.

***Day 32:***   Practice Exercise 24. Schedule your Initiation Ceremony for Day 40. Begin to prepare yourself.

***Day 33:***    Practice Exercise 25. Continue daily prepara-
            tions for Initiation until Day 40.
***Day 34:***    Practice Exercise 26.
***Day 35:***    Practice Exercise 27.
***Day 36:***    Practice Exercises 28 and 29.
***Day 37:***    Practice Exercise 30. Post your Manifesto where
            you can see it often. Revise it as appropriate.
***Day 38:***    Practice Exercise 31.
***Day 39:***    Practice Exercise 32.
***Day 40:***    This is the final day of the Forty Day Process.
            Prepare yourself reverently and perform
            Exercise 33.

This may seem like sort of a whirlwind experience
to you. If it goes too quickly, take as many days as you wish.
You may find that you spend four or five days on one
exercise before you feel like moving to the next one. Use
this as a guide, moving through it at the pace that best suits
you. Take at least forty days. Much of your growth is taking
place inside and needs a little time to take hold. Your
patience and persistence will pay off.

ଙ୍    ଙ୍    ଙ୍

In response to several requests for a daily routine,
I'm including what I call my "Daily Dozen." You can apply
each practice daily in a matter of minutes. Most of the
Practices can and should be used as you go through your
normal day. Enjoy these. Develop your own.

## *The Daily Dozen*

**Access:** Ask a question. Write the question at the top of the page. For the next ten minutes, write your answer to the question.

**Articulation:** Say something bold and wonderful about yourself each day — out loud. Say it several times during the day. (If you're in a crowded place, think it loudly.) Tell two people each day something specific you like about each of them. You may write a note to one of them, but you must verbalize the other.

**Intention:** Each morning write an Intention for the day. Use just one or two sentences. Write it on a card or in your planner — some place where you will see it.

**Visioning:** Each morning spend one to two minutes picturing the day ahead as if it were your ideal day. Really get into the feeling of it.

**Projection:** Creating the energy field between your hands, place one desire there and release it to the ethers.

**Allowance:** If something threatens to throw you off-center during the day, watch your reactions to it. Learn some affirmations, such as, "I allow only my good to come from this," or "This, too, shall pass."

**Focus:** Adopt a policy of being totally mindful of everything you do. Pay close attention to each detail.

**Forgiveness:** If you have a negative thought or feeling towards a person (including yourself) or a situation, remind yourself that, if you remove your negative energy from it, you can act from the highest position.

**Discipline:** Select one aspect of your life in which you will be disciplined, just for the day. Note how you feel at the end of a day in which you have successfully disciplined yourself in one area.

**Congruence:** Three times a day, ask yourself, "Is what I just did in congruence with my professed beliefs?" If the answer is, "No," change your behavior to the extent possible.

**World Service:** As many times as you think of it, ask Spirit, "What is the best use of my precious time and energy right now?" Act on your guidance.

**Initiation:** Each morning, as you shower, picture yourself being showered with a golden light. If you bathe, picture yourself in a pool of golden light. Before you go to sleep at night, ask that you be taken one more step on the path of initiation.

It is my sincere desire that you have a life of fulfillment, abundance and joy. You are a child of God and, therefore, worthy to inherit the Kingdom. Go in peace.

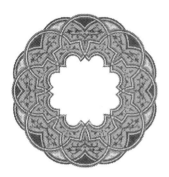

# Indexes

## *Index to Meditations*

## *Free Newsletter*

If you would like a copy of Pam Murray's newsletter, along with information about her many products and services to help you live a more successful life, please write her. She is very interested in learning of your experiences with this book and hearing about the practices you have developed for yourself.

Pam Murray

PO Box 1996

Walla Walla WA  99362

Fax (509) 522-1255

e-mail: PamMurray@aol.com

To order additional copies of:

# Remembering Your Destiny

Book: $14.95    Shipping/Handling $3.50

Contact:

**BookPartners, Inc.**
Fax: 1-503-682-8684
Phone: 1-800-895-7323